Wednesday

Dec 2005 Vol. 1 No. 3

the body and the blood

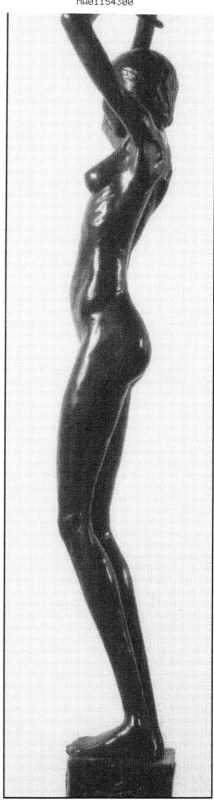

featured artist

joshu lucas

edited by

chiwan choi

judeth oden

writ large press

los angeles

COVER ART BY
Joshu Lucas

LAYOUT AND DESIGN BY
Judeth Oden

Contributing authors are members of the Los Angeles Poets and Writers
Collective. For information please contact: wednesdaymag@gmail.com.

letter from the editor

There are a lot of deaths here in the pages of "The Body And The Blood," Issue #3 of *Wednesday*. And where there isn't death, there's plenty of dying. No, we haven't gone Poppy Z. Brite goth or some turtle-neck pretentious, like this cafe in Los Angeles, on 6th near Alexandria, where there's a sign as you enter that says, "Where Art, Friends, and Angst meet." I know it's not that, even if I don't know what exactly it is that cycles through a community of artists, touching each and every member's life and work. Maybe it's just the time we are living through right now, with the war and the flood and the earthquakes and every other less glamorous tragedy in between. There are deaths in the writing because writers are cataloguing the events of their current world, just as writers and all other artists have done for centuries and centuries. But still, there's a part of me that says it's more than that. It's something more personal. It's like, trying to find some blank sheets of paper and a few pencil stubs on the burning desert surface of Los Angeles, we are merely discovering that everything is coming to an end.

Anyway, if I'm sounding more depressing than ever, don't mind me. But right now, I feel like not much in the world makes sense. We were recently given two 4 month-old Akita puppies. We named them Tu Fu and Li Po. A week later, Li Po stopped walking and we took her to the vet and watched the doctor pointing at bones on the x-ray where Li Po's spine was deformed, listened to him as he explained about excruciating pain and spinal surgeries that promised nothing. He left us alone for a few minutes so we could decide. What is there to decide?

Li Po is gone now, back to her mother waiting for somebody to decide something. So much changes everyday, life coming and going in a matter of minutes. And here we are, through all of it, trying to stay alive just enough to pick up a pen and put some words together.

In his poem, *Under The Dust*, Tim Silver writes about the deaths of his parents and his own unborn son: "Now a new boy/is coming, a son,/and I don't know/how to tell him/to sweep the dust/under the dust."

None of us do, but we just keep trying.

chiwan choi
editor

table of contents

conrad romo

PHANTOM PAINS

All in all, this has been the home to our family since the late 20's. I moved away 30 years ago and it was not so nice then and over this stretch of time it's aged poorly. Today we seem to all have a difficult time saying goodbye and getting this under way and done. There is a palpable sadness that clings like the ghosts among us. Call it a phenomenon, not unlike phantom pains that an amputee will experience, call it a variation of the battered wife syndrome, call it something like recidivism and the nearly impossible odds stacked against criminals like us to stay away from this unhealthy devil that we know so well. This will be it, once we are done with our tribute, our ceremony to ourselves, and our ancestors. Our cooking pots will be smashed, our bill paid in full, our stakes to our home pulled up, never to be visited again.

Rene drove in from Las Cruces. Jaime took the train in from San Diego. Letty lives just over in Eagle Rock, but no one knew for certain if she'd show up or not. Tessa had pretty much already moved out. Most of her shit anyway. She and Mari were pissed at each other again and weren't talking, but Rene heard from her to go on ahead with whatever we wanted to do without her. We are a two syllable lot, our family. There are the aunts: Mela, Pera, Bori, Becky, Marta, Anna, Molly. And uncles: Turo, Poncho, Pancho, Memo, Beto, Javie, Pedro, Tito, Weso and Tano. Just to mention a few. I shouldn't even start with the cousins: Tita, Chapo, Nejo, or Teecha. There are just too many. Because we have a lot of nicknames, sometimes the question is asked, "Hey what's Uncle Tano's real name?" This came up at his funeral. It took locating one of the *viejos* to find out it was Gaetano. Just this past week I discovered our mother's first name was Mary, and Lina, short for Evangelina, was her middle one. It was on her high school diploma that I found while helping to pack up.

So there we were, four of us at least, not counting dad, to do a final walk-through of the old homestead before it changed hands. I stood in the room where our mother fell to the floor and died of a heart attack and said thank you to her. My eyes welled up and I felt they could wash away with a torrent of tears if I started, so I didn't. Someone had gotten the idea that we needed a ceremony of some sort. A ritualistic farewell seemed fitting. Something short of a service, not so formal, but a pronouncement, an honoring. A gesture was required.

I brought a shovel. We agreed that we'd all put something in a can and bury it. Rene brought a tea tin that would seal tight enough. We weren't going for a time capsule.

We expected the contents to get wet, molder, and decompose in short order and we were fine with that.

A few of the things we buried: the crown of thorns removed from a bust of Christ that belonged to our grandmother, a small purse with pocket change, some frozen tamales that we made together last Christmas, some postcards that we all contributed, ashes from a pet, a snapshot of our younger family all laughing together so far removed from this day. We filled in the hole, burying the tin can with these contents and others that we kept private.

We fill in the hole and stamp the dirt down hard. I lay the shovel blade flat and Nena jumps up and down on it. We play the ceremony by ear, sharing memories until it feels forced.

One thing I meant to put in the can was a poem by Carver, the real short one that starts off, "and did you get what you wanted?" Later that day, I found a folded paper with the poem in my back pocket and I have no idea what it was that I mistakenly placed in the tin.

alicia ruskin

CORNER OF 46TH AND BROADWAY 1987

Through a double door
The door I hip checked open all night long
Always something in hand no wasted trips it's what you're taught
And get your own pen: be a professional
I owned more starched white shirts than fifty Wall Street punks
I could work burned cut hung-over
I learned about support hose at twenty-three, and speed.

Through that metal door rolled out the stink it's every kitchen in the free world
Four star to chicken shack
It's all the same you can't escape the
Rubber meeting mop juice tang
Hanging in the steam fried air with a top note of vinegar
And a finish of coffee grounds and grease
Gets in your blood like being paid in cash

Through that glass-eyed door tapped Mrs. Lee all 5 feet nothing
Tearing the line chef a new one in Chinese
He's slumped over a boiled duck its head discreetly turned
To avoid her cat skinning screed.
Now Mr. Lee we called Spot
An homage to the birthmark on his head the size of a loquat
Between shifts they sat their boys in matching blue blazers at the bar
We brought them ginger ale and Häagen-Dazs
It was the least we could do for making off with whole cheesecakes
And cases of paper towels.

Through that swinging door the back waiters all from Bayside via Kraków
Shouldered the weight of pre-theatre rush
They'd slipped through La Guardia with a fistful of doctorates but no papers
The best we called Chez the Engineer he'd stack a banquet tray

Eighteen covers high
Four hunan fish three jade filet and the rest whatever we could push
Probably the noodles
Brace it on his palm and put it right into the air
Nine feet above their gaping mouths a showstopper
La Cage Aux Folles next door had nothing on us

Through that shiny door my boys Danny Frank and Colin
Called themselves the Bitches of Eastwick
I'd do their sidework just to get the gossip first.
Unflappable gods of the upsell
Never in the weeds that I could see
The matinee ladies pimped out their spinster daughters
Despite the obvious
Years went by over rounds of Heineken
Frank moved back to KC when his mom broke her hip
Colin gave Danny the AIDS or was it the other way around

Sit down shut up eat tip get out
I had a dream
But that's a given.
Everything's gone now
Behind that impenetrable door.

.

caroline horton

HEAVEN: PART 1

I loved a man once, I still do. He told me, "Everything you need to be happy is in this room. You just need to look." He sat down in the cream leather chair and stared at me. His eyes were liquid pools. People often use that metaphor for eyes, but I have to say, they misuse it, in my opinion. His eyes really were liquid. Believe you me, when you looked into them, you reflected back distorted and upside down. "What you want is under the bed," he said, grinning.

It was the middle of our first deluge party. We lived in a huge square house with only three exterior walls. Where the fourth wall should have been there were four pillars and a terracotta-tiled patio that jutted out over the mountainside. It was hot all year round, and when it rained, it came down straight and narrow, the fastest point from cloud to peak. There was no wind. On the first Saturday of the rainy season we always had a big party starting around four in the afternoon when it was still light. He stood with his back to the invisible landscape, the light muted and barely purple, and toasted our friends. "To love!" he cried.

The smell of our house when it rained was exquisite. Chlorophyll seeped from the pores of the sodden leaves and, joining hands with the scent of the orchids and jasmine, would ride up on the mist that rose from the jungle floor and creep into our home as a wish, as a promise. I crawled under the bed. It was warm and sheltered and smelt of cherry wood and vanilla. The softness of friends' feet padding around barefoot was like a strange parallel heaven from here under the bed. I could see what it was, what he knew I was looking for: the book, just out of reach. The book was called *Fuck You And 101 Other Things I Like To Do*. It was a bizarre diary of sorts that we kept together. It was part journal, treasure hunt, photo album, notice board. We made at least one entry per day, no matter how small. It had leather binding and blank organic paper. Page one consisted of *I love you* written in twelve different languages, one for every hour. My favorite was six o'clock PM, Aramaic. I don't know why. We had photographs of the first snake that crossed our threshold unannounced, a baby python, and one the next day of the Shaman that came to protect our home from baby pythons. Never saw another. February 26th holds a splinter from a meteor that flung itself into our orbit, cascaded through light years and dropped into the arms of Poseidon in a place where we would eventually breathe underwater, sending bubbles skyward, fishy flippers flapping. November 10th, I believe, is a drawing of a tattoo I wanted. A white phoenix for the back of my neck. No one would do it. No joke. No one wanted to inject bleach into the spinal column. Can't blame 'em. May 5th, a photo of him on his birthday, naked on the bed wearing a huge goat mask. We wrote each other notes. The book became a manifestation of not only our life but also our love and, as such, took on the possibility of loss that was not hitherto present. It became my memory and my sense of danger. Looking back through its pages of beauty, I precariously balanced my future on it, convinced what lay ahead could not mirror what had gone before.

But nothing bad happened. The book just kept swelling and swelling until it was four times the size as when I got it. After three years together, it was so heavy and cumbersome you could no longer read it on your lap, so we had an altar built for it. The cover creaked now when you opened it. The clock of love had expanded so greatly, now encompassing twenty-four hours, that we had its image silk-screened and hung behind our bed. The bed was enormous; we'd had it made, as we spent so much time in it. The mattress was so god-damn soft that it leeched the pain, not only from your body, but I swear on the Bible, from your mind as well. We made love every day, even when we fucked, and if we did it on the side closest to the mountain at the bottom of the bed, I could stretch my arms far above my head into the rain and divert its path down my fingers, around my wrist, along my forearm, up over my shoulders and down between my breasts where it pooled for my lover. I never knew such bliss. I never templated my body under such devotion, I never cracked, I was seamless. And he smiled all day, every single day. I never saw him without a smile on his lips, kind and ingenious, or in his eyes. I never saw him be anything but gentle and full within his own space.

And I missed him this morning, years later, his mortal coil shrugged off long ago like damp breath fading from a mirror, and I missed the future I do not know, and I missed the memories I never lived. And his smile, I never miss his smile, because that became the shape of my love.

alan berman

THE INTIMACY PROJECT

Janice died Sunday.
She was almost my master teacher
when I did my practice teaching in 1989,
but she felt she needed more high school time
since she had just come up from the elementary levels.
She continued to treat her students like children,
but she got results: lots of state champions
and contest-winning writers.

She was diagnosed with lung cancer
on the first day of school
last year and given a short timeline.

I hate generalizations about dead people,
especially people I know well.
I'm glad I didn't go to the services today,
as there would be speech upon speech
of indigestible genuflection.

After we had been there a few years,
she and I collaborated
on a presentation to the department about
how to create poetry encounters for the students.
We put together poems we liked.
I had some Native American Indian pieces,
Adrienne Rich, some Emily Dickinson.
She never understood Dickinson, she said,
and wouldn't touch her.
I think she had a problem trusting perfection. I'll bet
she didn't own a dart board either.

Our preparation reminded me of the
rehearsals I used to have when I was in my other life,
my music life: I had great-looking flutists and
singers and did gigs with them throughout graduate school
and for years later.
When my friend Matt needed a flute player,
he asked our guitar teacher. Ted said, while in his 80s,
"Ask Alan—he has them on ice."
I heard of this remark only after Ted died.

I had fantasies about every one of those girls
and was probably too obvious about it.
Even then I knew that it was the intimacy
of preparation that was half the turn-on.
The back-and-forth of rehearsal and performance
is as close to sex as I was getting those days;
in some ways it's closer than some sex.
But none of them wanted anything to do with me
outside of the music. I wasn't a mensch yet—
I had to drop all my rushing after people
to finally get anywhere.

It would have been so great if Janice were physically attractive,
but she wasn't—she had a hysterical laugh,
a puffy face, a difficult figure.

We memorized Garrett Hongo's "Shakuhachi" poem
so that we could recite it in a simultaneous duet.
It's a long piece and I had a lot of confidence
in my reciting.

We had the 25 teachers
sit in the desks in the middle of the classroom.
By the time we got to this point in the presentation,
it was four o'clock and

we were all tired. These after-school
inservices are death-defying for everyone.
But we paced off from center, as though in a duel,
and turned to face each other from the opposite walls of the room.
We agreed to keep a steady walking pace
even as the poem changed rhythm,
that our voices would offer different nuances
as one of us was more easily heard than the other
by each teacher as we passed.
Everyone would have a fair chance
at the manifold blends of our voices.
We hadn't even figured out which direction
to start, we were so focused on the words.

We stepped to our right, proceeding counter-clockwise.
No one knew the secret of my flutes,
the poem starts,
and I laugh now, because some said I was enlightened.
We kept our eyes on each other to make sure
neither of us got ahead of the diameter line.
We had to keep the disc spinning at the same pace.
Classrooms are always rectangles, and we kept having
to break our circle for desks sticking out.
We got near the end and I lost the thread—
her eyes saw me wince and go limp inside.
She kept on moving and smiling and delivering the goods.
I caught up in a few words and only the teachers closest to me
knew I dropped out for those seconds.

It's not the failure that matters here,
it's her eyes that kept trusting that I'd get
out of that mess, that support she offered while I was
torturing myself for the mistake, the urging
in her movement for me to get past the defeat
to fulfill my responsibility.

maria cristina jiménez
WONDER WOMAN

Every day my looks lose patience and
slowly surrender into ordinary.
I no longer turn heads the way I used to.
I no longer get the catcalls, the whistles,
the hey baby, hey mama, hey *mami, mamacita,*
chula, rica, ven aqui, oohhh baby you're so hot,
oohh baby, hey baby, hey baby, look here, *mirame,*
look at me, in New York, in LA, in San Juan,
in Costa Rica, in Worcester, all over the world.
My identity used to rely on the male gaze:
men see me therefore I am.
Now I walk unnoticed, invisible, no matter what I wear.

"What is that outfit?" Mami asks.
It was one of those rare nights when I was gonna go out.
Usually I preferred to stay home reading
young adult novels, rather than hanging out
with young adults.
"I don't think so," she says as she eyes my miniskirt,
booking me on suspicion of *puta.*
"Let's go."

I hated this part. This was the part where
I had to cross the drawbridge,
looming over a moat replete with crocodiles,
and head toward my parents' bedroom.
This was the part where I would find Papi in
his underwear eating prosciutto.
This was the part where I had to model my dress
in front of him as mom stood beside like a silent gargoyle.
I would avoid his gaze as he stared down my legs.

He'd then ask me to turn around and as I did,
my hands stretched the traitor spandex to its limit.
I spun catching glances of myself in the wall mirrors.
I was Naomi, Linda, and Christy, sashaying down a Versace runway.
Nadia Comaneci finishing her series,
looking anxiously at Bela Karoly.
A frog in science class about to get dissected.
I let my parents scan my body with their X-Ray vision.
I wondered if they could see all the way to my insides,
past the smile, the sweetness, the forced goodness,
all the way towards the underground walls where
I'd grafittied my wrath. Papi told me the skirt was
indeed too short and that I had to go back and change.
I knew it was for my own good.
That he didn't want men looking at me
the way he had just looked at me.
I knew mom loved me and understood cause dad
didn't allow her to wear shorts or skirts.
I knew all that, but I didn't leave.
I kept turning.
I felt that if I kept twirling,
I could disappear like Wonder Woman
and end up somewhere else.

A PICTURE OF MY PARENTS

They were young, younger than I am now.
They hadn't had me or my brother.
He's wearing sunglasses.
She has thick eyeliner.
They look towards each other,
but their eyes don't meet.
He looks over her.
She looks past his right shoulder.
They smile, but hide their teeth.
She wears a blazer, ruffled shirt, skirt below the knee.
He's the thinnest I've ever seen.
His weight tilted onto his left hip.
His lower lip thicker than his top.
In all these years, I've never seen them kiss,
really kiss.

I fantasize that, after the photographer left,
he took mom in his arms and knelt.
He caressed the castle of her face.
She let him caress the castle of her face.
They laughed out loud.
They loved each other.
They were happy
before we came and their
island turned to water.

I take the portrait by its shoulder blades and shake it.
Shake it so much it almost breaks.
Shake it so much my parents in the picture
turn to look at me, overwhelmed.
"What are you doing?" they say.
"Stop it. What do you want us to do?" My father asks me
if I want him to look at mom. My mother asks me
if I want her to kiss dad.

They are worried.
They don't want me to suffer.

I tell them I want them to stay as they are.
That close. That apart.
I want my anger every time I look into that square.
My eyes squeeze so tight,
I can almost bring them together.
They smile, go back to their place
and my past, once more,
fits neatly inside my wallet.

christy dusablon

HAIR TODAY, GONE TOMORROW

I dated a guy who insisted that I shave my pubes off. Completely.

It's not that I mind the request, but this was not a request—

it was a make-it-bald-or-I-won't-touch-it thing.

Then he told me about his sex in the shower obsession.

The two exist as one event, apparently.

He also confessed that he'd had sex with an ex-girlfriend while she was on the rag.

"Okay," I thought, nothing odd about that.

But he continued with, "And after we were done,

I wrote my name on her back using my penis as the pen and her blood as the ink."

"Huh," I said, "well, art means different things to different people."

He was trying to shock me and it didn't work,

so he took my hand and put it down his pants.

I felt around.

Shaft. Check.

Balls. Check.

Circumcised. Check.

Pubes…pubes?

I felt all around that thing, looking for just one hair, just one.

He was smoother than a doorknob.

"So you trim," I said.

"No, I don't just trim, I get it all, all of it."

"You don't like hair, I get that, but you should know that I enjoy a little stubble.

It reminds me you're a man. It's comforting, I should say,

I mean not that I am opposed to the idea of being with a woman."

"You'd be with a woman?" he asked. "I am really not comfortable with that."

I didn't think much of it until he never called again.

.

HEMORRHOIDS ARE SEXY

"I think hemorrhoids are sexy."
"You think what?" I ask.
"Ya, they make me real hot."
"Hot as in sweaty or hot as in Brad Pitt in *Fight Club* hot?"
"Oh! *Fight Club* hot," she says.
Then she asks me if I've ever had hemorrhoids.
"I am not sure. I had an irritating itch that wouldn't go away,
but it only lasted about four and a half days. I think it was a fissure.
But it itched, man, it itched, and it wasn't sexy."
"Four and a half days. What's up with that?"
"I wondered the same thing," I say.

This girl is fantastic. She's such an actress with all her sexy hemorrhoid talk;
no one really thinks hemorrhoids are sexy.
She's fooling with me, but this is the most intellectual conversation
I've had in hours, days even.
I've been sitting around watching re-run after re-run of *Friends*
for the past four hours.
Then this girl comes along.
She's my neighbor, only I didn't know it.
She moved in because the girl that occupied the apartment before her
thought the kitchen was too small, so she left.

"Lucy, do you smoke pot?" I ask.
"Let's talk about dandruff," she yells.
"Uh, okay, what about it?"
"Do you get it?" she asks.
"Only if I don't wash my hair for a couple of days,
but I don't own Head 'N Shoulders, if that's what you're getting at."
"Oh," she says. "That's lovely news."

JUST A COUPLE MORE

He walks with me for a while. It's all I really want,
especially on a night like this.
It's crisp and almost Halloween, fall's culmination.
A spider could crawl across my hand and I wouldn't know the difference.
It is finally cold outside.
I cupped my hands and blew hot lung air into the middle.
He is not handsome, but he reminds me of a boy I knew when
I was about thirteen. The boy lived a couple blocks away.
He'd come over to my street and complain about his mother.
He was someone I liked very much, but could never envision loving.
My new companion complains in the same fashion,
but about parking in Los Angles and waiting in line.
He is simple and we have no attachment to one another.
It's easy to find things to talk about.
I walk with him and think of Christmas
and the smell of my folk's house when the tree is up.
I think of peeling oranges and of the new bike I wanted
so badly and got.
I think about how I am happy now,
away from the debauchery,
away from my father, the drunk,
away from my mother and all her fragile nature.
I think about how I don't miss things the way I thought I would.
We walk a little farther and I ask him to walk just a couple more blocks.
He tells me about the past couple years of his life
and I hope that I am making a friend.
It's been a while since I've wanted one.
We walk a couple more blocks and then he drops me beside my door.
"Well, I'll see you sometime," I say.
I wave
and he waves back.

LOVE SICK

I've been sick for four days now.
My body, for the time being, is not mine.
It coughs and sneezes and I am just a visitor.
Julian, the man in my life, has been taking care of me.
He makes me tea and grabs the Kleenex.
He's become my body's best friend.
For a long time, I've felt like a visitor in his life,
but here, like this, it's like we're finally standing still.
I am comfortable, at peace even.
The room is sound
and my body lies wrapped and medicated in his bed.
He's not with me, but I don't mind.
Everything in this room is his,
but I don't feel like an intruder.
I press my head against his pillow.
I can't smell him, but I imagine all of his scent.
Etherized,
I begin to burden myself.
I am, I am, traumatized and itching off my dead skin.
I pick it from under my fingernails
and resume italicizing sentence after sentence.
I am not sure that there is any difference between being awake and being asleep.
I can feel his hand on my head.
It's cold.
He kisses my forehead and presses the covers tight all around me,
the way my mother used to do.

SOMETHING NEW, SOMETHING OLD, SOMETHING USED, AND SOMETHING BLUE

"One drink," he'd said.

"Oh, I dunno," she'd replied, shifting back and forth from one foot to the next.

"It's a celebration! Just one drink between a couple of old friends."

He hadn't even finished his pep talk before they'd taken the first sip.

It hadn't taken but a half hour before she was paralyzed, comatose, prey.

"So what happened?" I asked from the top bunk.

She was below me, safe on the bottom bunk.

We'd just met, she and I. We'd shared one very short, very basic,

"hello-good-bye-what's your favorite food-color-please tell me you're neat-not messy-I think

we could be friends" conversation.

Both of us, third-year college students,

wanting everything from an "A" to a drunk back seat in some van

on its way to some football game.

Only here she was, my very new acquaintance, illuminating her darkest secrets

in a very dark room to me.

I am not sure whether it was her bravery

or the sheer fact that I was uncomfortable, but I'd never felt meeker.

I knew what happened, but I had to ask.

I knew he took half of every part of her,

but I had to ask.

"I woke up," she said.

"I woke up and put my clothes back on,

and nothing has been the same since."

SACRIFICE

"I am not sure if she remembers me, but I don't have the heart to ask,"
she said.

My mom's voice sounded so close,
but I knew she was miles away.
The plane dropped her in Winnipeg, Canada. Her hometown.
She's 47
and this is the first time she's traveled alone.
It's things like this
that make me wonder what she's been doing all this time.
My great grandmother is 95.
Both her body and mind are disintegrating.
She's barely a reflection of what she once was.

"She remembers you," I said.
"Maybe not everything, but she remembers you."

We got off the phone and I thought for a while
about the things people sacrifice.

AN OCCURRENCE IN A PARK

I drive into the sun,
past the gate and into a spot.
There are trees, lots of trees.
I try to remember the park before
the trashcans
and community bathrooms,
before the benches and the road,
a time when nature was whole,
forbidden to any who couldn't handle it.
I sit and wonder if I am
one of those people,
afraid to be part of something significant.
The pen runs out and my thoughts seem to go with it.
It's not enough
just to be alive.

tim silver

UNDER THE DUST

In the shed
behind the house
I sweep the dust
across the cement floor.
Gray family footprints,
crushed in its pores,
stand up in clouds
to meet me,
clutch my throat,
turn my hands' blood
black and dry.
Gripping the broom
hard, hard as I can,
its painted handle yellowing
my blistered palms,
I sweep to the end,
find the edge
where bones crack,
shake away my hands,
imagine all the dust
swept clean.
As a boy,
only slowly
could I imagine
the night my mother died
had come true.
My father watched,
he knew,
and reached across
my questions
to cover my eyes.

One year ago,
I stood by my mother's grave
to lay his dust
into the ground
beside her.
Now a new boy
is coming, a son,
and I don't know
how to tell him
to sweep the dust
under the dust.

carrie white

WHISH WISH

Oh my God, if I could only express the feeling of excitement I get when I hear a song from the 70's that I used to roller-skate to, or see a skater speed across the rink and do some fancy leg work. Top that off with a disco ball spinning around the room, and I tell ya', I just wanna' burst. That's my ball game, my sex, my lover. I remember my wonderment as a child watching the big kids and then getting my first pair of skates. There was power that came with having my own skate-key hanging on a string around my neck, feeling my wings grow as I was able to lift my weight with a tiny leap over the sidewalk cracks and not fall. Skating was independence flowing through my veins, my private freedom. Skating was my escape long before the fun of private clubs with Cher in Reseda and *Flippers* on La Cienega. Skating is a place I go in my head, a world of my design, with fresh air, where I am protected and my spirit is never down—whish, whish, the sound of me skating past all my troubles. I escape from my house and my stepfather, that perverted drunken twisted psycho maniac bastard. Where I could skate over his body like the toughest bitch in the Red Devil's Roller Derby, slam him into the cement walls of the dome, squash him into bloody broken bits with my wheels like he ripped out my innocence with his disgusting dick shoved down my throat, down my gagging throat, down my dreams of a happy, peaceful, safe life at home, down my hopes that each day would bring a new beginning. I take a big breath of fresh air and move to other places (whish, whish), the best, most fun times of my young adult life, skating in my spandex pants to my favorite disco music and never wanting it to end. I worked in my hair salon on roller-skates. I drove my car in my roller-skates.

Then I fell. I prefer to think of the fun, but I can't ignore the major fall, the kind that creeps in and everything ends broken. My roller-skating was no longer about independence. It was about irresponsibility. I was losing my bearings and not the ones in my wheels. I couldn't ignore that my world was falling apart. I couldn't ignore me. I wanted to skate through my life without being hurt. I wanted to be left alone and have crowds around me. I wanted to skate in the clouds and swing on the shimmering light-reflections of the disco ball. I didn't want to feel the ground swallowing me up as I lost control. I still have my skates from *Flippers* in my garage. They would say about me, "She's not a great skater but she takes the corners like a Porsche." I am indebted to skating like to an old friend, a partner, a teacher, a competitor. My average skating talent enhanced my ambitious imagination. Today I delight in watching my grandchildren investigate themselves through their skating, trying to balance and challenge their skills, competing with personal pride, all assets for greeting life and, of course, the fun of it all. And the mirrored ball in my mind starts spinning. I'm not through yet. I'm strong and want to rollerblade with my iPod into the sunset on the Venice Beach path, skating against time, firming my ass, and taking that big breath past my throat to my ankles.

---

francine taylor
STOLEN GOODS

We stole them from the neighbor's tree back then,
age ten to maybe fifteen,
every fall,
over a cyclone fence
to lift ones that had fallen into leaves
moist from the change of seasons.
These were crisp and tasted of
sneakiness
because we were too dumb
to ask the kind minister
for permission to eat
down to the core.

Years later, his wife told us
they knew all the time
and saw us scrambling over the fence
to grab the fruit quickly,
pears of an unknown variety
hanging heavy on the branches
or lying at our feet,
then pulling ourselves over the fence,
with *Keds* sneakers just barely fitting
into the diamond shaped metal fence holes,
safely back in our own yard
with the fruit of our labors,
crunchy, soft,
sweet, unwashed
stolen goods.

I have since learned that

many varieties exist
beyond Bartlett:
Starkrimson,
Asian brown,
Bosc,
Concord,
D'anjou,
yellows, greens, reds, browns,
thick skins,
thin skins,
firm,
soft,
bruised.

amy slomovits

PENELOPE THE PEOPLE PLEASER DOLL

I dry humped my way through high school.
Health class weighed heavy on me.
If I had a denim barrier, I felt safe.
I didn't want no stinkin' herpes, gonorrhea, AIDS, syphilis, babies,
or boys who didn't know how to let go of my teat.
I thought once I let them inside, they'd never leave.
Better to tease and lure, lure and tease.
The juice is in the lure.

Make them want me,
then test them to see if they want me bad enough,
but not too bad.
Make them want me,
then push them far so they will come close,
but not too close.
Make them want me,
then peel off their clothes,
but not mine.
Make them want me,
then touch him,
but not me.

I'll please him till his eyes roll back in his brain,
just pull the string
and I'll tell you something you want to hear.
I'll never wet.
I'll eat for your pleasure.
I'll cry on cue.
I'll shit on myself before I shit on you.
I'm Penelope,
I'm Penelope the People Pleaser Doll.

thomas natick

SHIVA

The stitches in my lips
laced my soul like an albino octopus.
As I raised my crutches to the church bell,
she cracked open my oyster shell heart,
sucked the pearls from my skull.
reached inside me
and drank the pain.
She let it fill her belly.
Only then did she
know me,
did she see me,
love me,
betray me,
only then could she
forget me.
Never before have I stood so silent.
Frozen
in a strait jacket of razor blades.

I longed to fly like a winged alarm clock
shattering the veil of reality,
ringing the stars like doorbells.
Finally, I rose
up, up, up,
my toes elongating,
forcing me heavenward through the void
until I pierced the belly of the moon,
where the melted plasma of a trillion mosquitoes
dripped from my eyes like honey.

This is always the way.
Perhaps it's genetic,
predestination,
to sit beside my empty snail shell
waiting for a new housekeeper,
the mouth of time closed around me,
leaving me like a hairless kitten in the dark.
Alone,
I treaded the pinecones
ripping at the stitches,
groping at the razor blades,
wrestling with the octopus,
trying to shake myself free from the puzzle.
Trying to empty the sandbox
and demolish the castles
and burn the Dixie cups,
until I could soar like a dove
from the ashes of her belfry
to singe my wings on the fringes
of the universe.

chris kerr

THE BUS RIDE

Grammy taught us how to take the bus from our house on Genesee Street to Hollywood Boulevard. On our first trip, we went to the Pantages Theatre to see *Black Christmas*. Even though we protested, telling her we didn't want to see a scary movie, she insisted a suspenseful thriller would be fun, and pointed out that one day we'd probably go to college and this would be a way for us to see how college girls really live. "Yeah," I said, "I read in the paper that it's about sorority sisters getting murdered."

"Well, that's just make-believe. Remember, it's only a movie."

I knew our bus was approaching because "91W HOLLYWD BLVD" was printed in big block letters over the driver's head. I noticed he had skin the color of coffee with cream, and a shiny pink scar on his chin, as if someone hooked him real good, and he wore a New York baseball cap that didn't cover the weary look in his eyes. Grammy stood alone like a limb and waited. I wondered if she felt old like a tree—like, if I counted her rings, would she be older than we knew? Grammy started to hand the exact change to the driver, but he pointed to the till and we listened as Grammy dropped the quarters, nickels and dimes down the chute, and I heard Cynthie say, "It sounds like Las Vegas."

Kitty sat next to Grammy. Cynthie and I sat next to each other. I had the window seat on the way to the movie on condition that Cynthie would have it on the ride home. Every time the bus stopped with a sudden jerk it shook Grammy from a daydream or some kind of far-off meditation. I could never figure out what she was thinking, her pale blue eyes always milky as though she'd given in to the same desperate thought or hopeless dream or broken promise; like inside she was sorry because she couldn't be all the things she wanted to be. She had survived my grandfather who died when dad was six, and then her second husband disappeared. I never met him, but I overheard Aunt Burdee telling Mother he was nothing more than a drunk. She said that one Christmas Harry drank so much eggnog that, when he was putting an ornament of Baby Jesus on the tree, he knocked the whole thing over, and then fell right on top of it and got tangled in its branches. Grammy never quite forgave Harry because she never had much to offer the boys and he'd spoiled her one big surprise.

I've inherited Grammy's first name, but I don't want to inherit her place in this world. Whenever she caught me staring at her, she'd say, "Take a picture. It lasts longer."

And I'd say, "I wasn't staring, I was thinking."

"Well then, *think* facing a different direction."

Grammy didn't look like other passengers on the bus. She was overdressed and stood out as if she were deliberately trying to embarrass me. Her pink polyester pantsuit had gone out of style at least ten, but probably more like twenty years earlier. The pink and white knitted beret she wore covered her thin fading carrot-colored hair and appeared handmade. Her red and white chiffon blouse had been worn so many times the pattern had started to fade. Her white nurse's shoes were thick like cheese, and when she sat down I could see her ankles looked like Italian sausages wrapped in sagging nylon packages.

The bus traveled east on Sunset Boulevard and I tried breathing out of my mouth to avoid swallowing the smell of dirty feet followed by unwashed greasy skin. I was careful not to get too close to the leftover face marks or maybe it was Crisco plastered on the window beside me.

Cynthie stared straight ahead and played with her fingers. I wanted to ask her if she ever dreamed we'd end up like this—on a bus without a mother, but with a mean grand-mother who decides what movies we were to see, what television shows to watch, what food we were to eat, what time to go to bed, what time to wake up in the morning, what clothes to wear (even on Saturday), the houses we were not allowed to ride our bikes by (Ricky's, Bobby's, John's), how short or long we were to wear our school uniforms. Grammy chose the friends we could invite over for a sleepover and then she'd call, "Lights Out. And I don't want to hear a peep out of any one of you or your girlfriends will go home." She'd say this before we had the chance to share our ghost stories or perform our séances or try the stiff-as-a-board-light-as-a-feather levitations. Grammy decided what time to go to mass on Sun-day and how long we were to talk on the telephone. She decided the rules and what punish-ments we deserved.

As the bus turned left on to La Brea Avenue, I tried asking Cynthie. She had her fists in a ball, her thumbs held captive under her whitening knuckles. We turned right onto Hol-lywood Boulevard and I tried not to notice she has Mother's fingers.

I swallowed a hiccup and the smell of the 91W bus and tried asking Cynthie through the space between my teeth if she ever dreamed, but only a little sound escaped.

When we reached Highland Avenue, I couldn't help noticing Hollywood Boulevard was the color of bad weather; the green and red Christmas lights; the hanging wreaths bound with red ribbon looking out of place against an almost blue sky; the street dressed in hand-me-down clothes that didn't quite fit. I asked Grammy if we could get off and walk the rest of the way.

"No," she said, "The theatre is miles down the road."

"Yeah, but I want to look for James Dean's star."

"I want to look at the stars, too," Kitty said.

Grammy wouldn't budge. She just repeated that it was too far to walk and added that she was afraid we'd miss the beginning of the movie.

"You said you used to walk five miles on your knees, in the snow, to church every Sunday."

"That's enough, Tess."

"But, Grammy, I want to find James Dean's star. He's my hero and the love of my life."

"He's dead. And don't think I won't give you a knuckle sandwich, right here in front of everyone. Just settle down." Grammy spit under her breath.

The bus hummed past cracked sidewalks sprinkled with ghosts and crippled saints, the freak and the guitar player and the bag lady and the wrinkled man and the lovers and the mortal sinner, the venial sinner and the cowboy, the dirt and the paradise and the world within a world. There wasn't a person on the bus who cared if Grammy slapped me across the face or, as she put it, gave me a knuckle sandwich.

Shit had become my favorite word. I'd say it in my head over and over and over. I'd say it out loud when no one was listening. I'd say it with my friends. I'd say *shit* not only when I was mad, but to explain the way I felt. I wondered what I said before I discovered *shit*. "Grammy," I wanted to say, "You make me feel like shit." She always had her way; even Dad seemed to give into her.

Cynthie and Kitty stayed out of my conversation with Grammy. Cynthie continued to stare and played with her fingers. Kitty leaned in close to Grammy—almost touching her shoulder—as if Kitty needed to cuddle, but was afraid to get too close. I guess we all were afraid. I was afraid. Dad was afraid. Mother was afraid. I don't know about Uncle Bud and Aunt Burdee or my cousins Scottie, Heather and Lauren—I don't know if they were afraid. Maybe I was afraid because I was always in trouble with Grammy. In trouble for not eating pea soup, for not eating liver, for not drinking milk, for not eating tomatoes, for not going to bed on time, for taking an extra donut after church, for talking on the phone too long, for not moving as fast as she liked when she called my name. "Tess, come in here and clean up the breakfast dishes," or "Tess, go upstairs and check to see what your sisters' bedrooms look like, and while you're up there, clean your own damn room and clean the bathroom. The toilet should sparkle. I want to eat my lunch off the bathroom floor."

When Grammy gave me a look, her eyes told me she didn't like me, and when I looked back at Grammy, my eyes were saying: I'm not afraid of trouble.

kate crash

THE GARANTULA

I can smell him on me
Like the way I wear death
It's a skeleton I can feel
All over myself
Like when I was thirteen and I was so close to the end
My family still gets shivers when someone speaks of those years and I don't even have to be mentioned in 'em for the grimness of grey and rain to come over their eyes
The way I was always so trapped inside and tryin' to find a sharp enough shape to cut myself away from...
And I wore death I felt the skeleton of myself when I was so far gone on various guns of little pills and shots and mind blown
But I now, I just smell him on me
And he smells so good
Like the smell of fresh blood in the morning I ate a cow once before it was fully dead, felt its heart beat when I reached inside his chest and on the farm where i grew up
Oh shutup
It's really not that bad
Okay
Okay
I'll stop here now why
'cause I can

MY AUNT

Her hand is soft and wet like silver
Drops in the morning
Collecting on the tip of the flower
That is no longer yellow
But dried and ready to be swallowed
Whole by the ground
In decomposition
An act of poetry
She reaches for me,
Lying there falling
Petal by petal
I watch her smothered into a blanket of white
Beep beep. beep beep. beep beep.
beeeeeeeeeeeeeeeeeeeeeeeeeeeeeeeeeeeeeeeeeeeeeeeeeeeeeeeeeeeeeeeee
Flatline
Beeeeeeeeeeeeeeeeeeeeeeeeeeeeeeeeeeeeeeeeeeeeeeeeeeeeeeeeeeeeeeeee
And although I never took her hand before
[I can almost feel as]
She reaches for me no more.

AHHH FAMILY

AAhhh, Family…
Sooooo,
Soooo
So-sooooo
So0looohh
So 0hhhh

Ode to mom.
Ow my stomach, my pancreas…my tennis court

Ode to dad/
Hello drink.

Ode to re'
Something stinks

Ode to alex, my brother…alex
Ping pongs and ice cream and playin' bats in front of the tv and and and I wish he'd pay me
back all that money he owes me

Ode to eric. Yes everyone's related another brother
Nothing to say. what? No, don't relate

Wade
Disappeared.

Ann
Gay and hating

Lynn
No, she don't like me

Mary
Ran when she can

Uh, uh, who else?
Marcheta
The cheetah, no not really, she had a peg leg and now lives in cincinnati

Husband's name is joe
He's no schmo but I wouldn't know...the last five were my dad's kids from his first cock fizz,
oops, fix, and
And
And
They don't talk to me none

Ann
Yes. My mom's a lesbian.
British.
No sex
Sweet
And very british

Dianne
I can't did you know that I can't believe that my dad was fucking his next girlfriend and
prostitutes before he left my mom, but she was fucking another girl...I wish she didn't fuck
me over with my money, but at least somebody loved me

Julia, maria, marta, lupe, ahhh yes not ken
Great fucking moms/maids.

Me.
Terrible lonely wretched happy singy smelly little beast

You.
Wanna screw?
Fuckin' jew,,,

No.
Outside.
The lights don't shine…
No…
Not quite right
I gotta twitch in my eye…
It says goodnight.

robert carroll

CROSSING CHASMS

I got a call from my sister today to tell me things aren't well.
She has to go to Michigan to consult with a doctor about having a colostomy
because of the scarring from the radiation after the surgery, but that's not why she called.
She's having an exacerbation of the same undiagnosable lung and skin disease
she had a few month ago, and she's having trouble catching her breath.
"The kids are running around the house so we have to be brief," she tells me.
She doesn't know if her husband will be able to go to Ann Arbor with her,
so I offered to go if she needs me. "O.K." she says and, "We'll talk next week."

I get off the phone and read a poem from Christy about her sister who is beautiful, but
scared and sad. Her sister is trying to solve things on her own and it's making Christy have
visions of beauty and ugliness.
So, now I sit at my desk and write about my own sister, also younger than me,
And how I wasn't there for her when we were kids
And how…
And now, how fifty years later, it's different.

SILVER MY HAIR

It's another one of those nights. What to do. What to do.
Write poetry, masturbate. Watch television, masturbate.
Masturbate, watch television. Masturbate, masturbate, masturbate.

You know that thing where women are supposed to want
their men to be poets. I'm a poet. Where's it gotten me?

You know the silverback gorilla?
They don't even get to be silverbacks
until they're getting laid regularly.
Help me make the hormones flow.
Help me silver my hair.

THE TRUTH

From her breast cancer
To her grief
To his manic depression
To his suicidal thoughts
To the meeting at the bistro
Where they laughed
And promised each other
They would call
Before either took their own lives
But the twinkle in her eyes was a lie
And the twinkle in his meant goodbye

THE GREATER HEARTLESSNESS

As soon as I saw her lean toward me
 eyes open wide—
a man could fall down through his own knees
        for those eyes—
Her lips aquiver—
I could feel the buzz of my body,
her voice in my ear.
        Her tongue…

Listen, I could tell you about
        the times
        I fell hard
and the times I just fell.
I could tell you about love
        in the rocky chasms
of the last forty years
and the glory of horns
        when we flew.
But I wouldn't be doing you
        any favors,
so I will stay with the truth.

I have lived. I have died. I have
        been blessed,
but with each lost resurrection came
a greater heartlessness.

EXACTLY WHAT SHE WANTS

Question: Why do men die before their wives?
Answer: They want to.

My wife wants me to take care of her during her terminal illness,
assuming she *gets* one.
Then she wants me to kill her if and when she's ready to go.
This is what love has come to.

I want to have my ashes strewn off Point Lobos just south of Carmel.
It's the only place I've found where I'd like to spend eternity—
        except maybe Hawaii.

One of my patients gave his wife a cocktail after she'd been a quadriplegic
for eight years. She asked him to do it. Talk about right to life.
        She earned her right to die.

But only one of us can go first, so if it has to be my wife,
it would be my pleasure to mix the drugs.

It will be the last time I can give her
exactly what she wants.

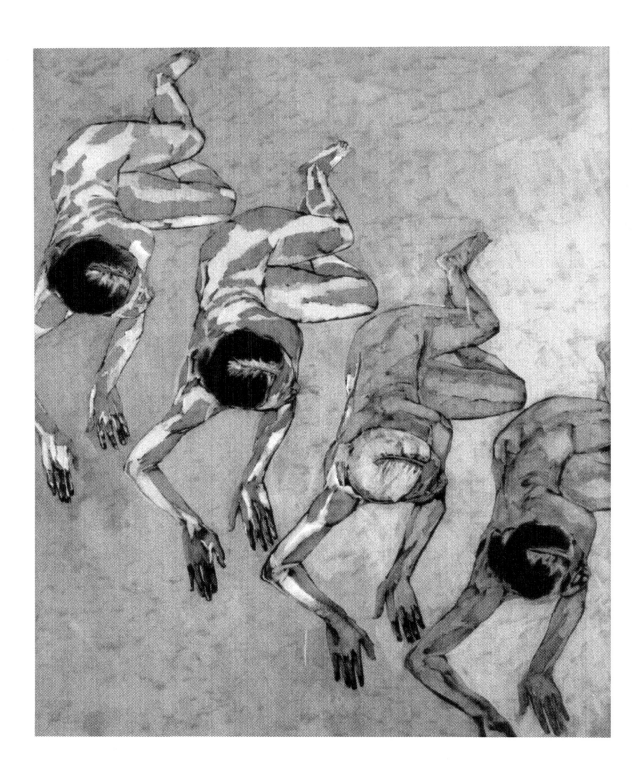

marguerite lambrinos

JOURNAL—OCTOBER 2, 2005

I hate October in Los Angeles. Back where I come from, in October the air smells cooler. Your toes chill in summer sandals. The leaves really do turn yellow and red instead of dusty green. I mean, like you can say, "There's fall in the air." Here in LA, all you can say is, "There's smoke in the air." I flick the AC back on so my eyes don't water and watch the hillsides spring into flames and burn orange, bubbling down to black like the bottom of a burnt pot. The fall colors of LA, orange, black, ending at a line of green grass and a blue pool and a big white house on the edge. Ashes to ashes, dust to dust. Maybe next time the white house won't be so lucky. The winds will roar and the embers will catch and the house will sizzle and pop and melt to the ground—in seconds, over, over in seconds. All the decoration and gleaming wood floors and recessed lighting and Corian counter tops, all the chic will dissolve back to the black earth. I wonder about all the time, the hours spent with decorators or in Home Depot on Saturdays, or searching the Internet for just the right piece of furniture. Is all that wasted time?

I'm kneeling in my own field of lost dreams in the dining room of the house I lived in for seven years with my husband of 32 years. I stopped counting after 32 because that's when I left, three years ago, and moved to a tiny place up in the canyon. So I'm back in the dream house, the one I call *La Casa Grande*. I've been back many times before because we have a handicapped son to care for. I was so entangled with this man and this place. I know the water pressure in the kitchen faucet is low and that it takes a long time for the water to get hot. I know the garbage disposal is sensitive and the toilet in the master bath doesn't always flush correctly and the brass doorknob on the front door sometimes wiggles loose and comes out in your hand like a monster's big gold tooth. I know I couldn't stand living with the man anymore. The man was mean—abusive, they call it now. This is the place where I finally grew up, stood up, opened up my eyes and saw that domineering man shrivel into a little boy whining in the corner about everything bad I did or didn't do to make his life the way he thought it should or shouldn't be.

So I'm kneeling on the Oriental rug he sent back from Turkey when he was there in Desert Storm. Does anyone remember that war? I remember I missed him. Can that be? I missed him? I'd listen on the radio all the way home from work to hear the latest news from Iraq then run in the house and turn on the TV. A Reserve Unit eating lunch in a mess hall near the airport hit by a SCUD missile. A letter from the man that same day saying he often ate at a barracks near the airport. Fire and burning bodies and casualties. Was the man there? Was he in that fire? This was when we lived back East where the air is always cooler in October and leaves always turn crimson and yellow and always fall in layers and layers on the lawn; soft, wet leaves melding back to earth.

I'm holding a fistful of silver forks and spoons. Silver place settings. I think I picked the pattern out with my mom. The silver is dirty, tarnished a chalky gray. I write down how many on a piece of paper and wonder how much they are worth. The lawyer said that this was the hard part, filling out all the forms. We are in the section that says to list all the furniture, china, silver, jewelry. I've put this off for three years. The only way to do it is to do it. The lawyer is no help. I asked him how to figure out how much furniture is worth. He answered for about five minutes and it all sounded pretty logical, but then I realized I had no idea what he said and less idea what to do. That was last week. This week he sent me a bill for $250,000. I hate lawyers. It's like doctors. You tell them all the symptoms and they look at you like you're crazy and then they draw on their extensive training and expertise and say, "You need to lose weight."

The man of *La Casa Grande* says, "What are you doing?"

I'm trying to fill out this list that we've had for two years, you know, the one that my lawyer said we had to fill out as a first step to get a divorce, the list that, if we do it together and do it all nice and civilized, will be easier for everyone and cost everyone the least amount. You know, this list that we talked to the lawyer about last week. Remember last week? Let's see, was it Tuesday or Wednesday? You were there, weren't you? I just got the bill from the lawyer yesterday. You know, the reason I came over here at 7:30 tonight after a hard day's work. Oh, that's right, you never thought teaching was much of a job, did you? I forget so easily. So where is your list?

The man says, "Uh, uh, I don't know." In the car maybe? Listen, I'm traveling this Thursday. Can you take Miguel and then pick him up at his recreation program? Sure, sure. Can you go out to the car and get the list so we can compare them? The man looks at me. No, we need to sit down and talk about this before we put things down on paper. The man says this as he paces back and forth.

Good, good. That's why I'm here tonight, remember? I pull out the teak and rope chair next to me at our teak dining table that sits 8 to 10 people without the leaf in, the one we first bought back east in the spring in Washington, D.C., when the cherry blossom buds were ready to burst open. I wonder how much it cost then? How much does it cost now? Who the fuck cares? I do, I think.

Have you ever been weeding in your garden? You know, not just surface weeds, but the ones that go deep. You pull and you pull. You get a hold of a big mothersucker and pull. It breaks off and you fall back, dirt in your eyes and mouth and the damn weed is still there, its fresh cut insides glaring back at you. Getting a divorce after a long marriage is a little like that, I think. I don't really know. I have no experience with this. I've never done it before. I'm the first in my big Catholic family to do it.

The man of *La Casa Grande* doesn't sit down in the teak chair next to me. I guess he didn't literally mean sit down and talk. He concedes by leaning over the chair and squinting at the list. I want you to know that there are many things on this form to fill out. List all our properties, our bank accounts and numbers, our employments, IRA's, 401k's, CD's. But for some reason the man must see the word "jewelry" in big letters. JEWELRY. "What did you do with all the JEWELRY?" he says.

I stare at a lighter spot on the teak table and wonder if it could be sanded out and refinished. I look at my empty ring finger, the one with the permanent ring-scar line and wonder where I put my wedding ring. My earlobes get hot and burn and I feel the clogs where I let the skin fill in the holes where earrings used to dangle. JEWELRY! Some old rotten taste seeps into my mouth. Some old churning in my stomach, some simmering pot of old stew that sat on the stove too long. JEWELRY! My eyes burn like gems in the night. I thought that you gave them to me as gifts. Gifts! I tell him how ugly they all were (they aren't). He tells me I must be tired. Oh, you think! Why are you yelling? We need to sit down and talk this over. Sit, sit. I was sitting. I can't believe this is happening again, me disintegrating right before my own eyes. Fine, fine, you can have all your fucking JEWELRY back. You decide how much it's worth and you keep it. I slam the door, go to the car, roll down the windows. I start to cry, but without much emotion or pain. Just exasperation. I've done this all too many times before. I know how the movie ends. The Santa Ana winds blow through the car, but my flare-up is starting to lie down. Lie down in the dark and scorched earth, smell the embers, smell the black, wait for the winter rains to wash away the soot, keep your eyes open for the new shoots sprouting. Don't waste your tears, except to water the new life.

kathy graf
THE ANGEL OF LIFE

I kiss his shoulder and watch his hand clench. It looks painful, atrophying inside itself. I run my fingers through his hair and feel the spastic twitch of his head. It must be exhausting. Here, I will breathe warmth onto this tired neck. I will lick this ear and whisper inside it.

He groans. A show of vulnerability so rare for this man. This slick Beverly Hills lawyer. This man who thinks his money is so attractive. This man who can't look me in the eye. I was going to take him out to lunch today. Instead, I brought lunch and he brought wine and we're in some apartment in Santa Monica his wife doesn't know about. I haven't the foggiest idea why I came. Or rather, it is so complex, I don't have it in me to sort it through.

I use my nails gently on his back. He has set the unspoken rule. As long as I don't look at his face, I should do whatever I want. It is at once a feeling of sexual power…and sexual humiliation.

I move my tongue down the crack of his ass. So thin now. So destroyed. All his bravado can't hide the truth of this naked body. A body slowly petrifying, becoming its very own tomb. A body I want very much to restore. It's not his money that attracts me. Nor the wine cellar he showed me last time. I'm not a woman to be bought. When I choose to act the whore, I do it on my own nickel.

He mumbles, "You're killing me, you're killing me." No, sweet baby, no. It's not me who kills you. It's not me who takes your life one muscle at a time. Rendering useless limbs. Dashing simple liberties. Robbing your body of its right to be still. It's not death that I offer, my dear man. My tongue slides downward. I am the Angel of Life.

I say a silent prayer to my husband. Don't be looking down from wherever you are and see us here. It would upset him. But then again, my husband didn't go through the grief of his death like I did. He didn't have to fight his way back to life like I did. Who had to rage and go mad and come back again? I did! I did! Hot-tear, white-fire fear that ate me every day. Teeth marks, crunching, tearing, ripping a hole in the center of my gut. Mock me. Laughing at my lack. Lackey lacks. Idiot girl. Dead brain. Trying to think up words and poof! Dictionary. Symmetry. Analogy. Fart. Look it up. Chastise and misspell, mispronounce. Fuck you and your fucking memory. Some of us have to pay to drink in this town. Some of us have to fall down the fucking well before we're allowed to swallow. Swallow me brain geek. Let me suck up and rip off your swamp of knowledge and know how. Puke me back again.

Righteous ingrates, what do they know? Have to be pumped. Pumped and seething. Gut twirling eyes red. Anger on my fingertips. Hating you and him and how dare he die and back to that place of madness. Hair-pulling audacity. Revisit the ugly ache. Pecking. Nails scratching little white boxes. Beating. Arms of metal, teeth clenched, biting bullets of spit and disgust. You died and I write. You in dirt, me hanging on a clothesline. Pounding my keys. Pounding my heart. I got kids motherfuckers! I got kids and they got eyes and they look at me and they show me this. World gone wild at seven years old. Scratched. Snuffed. Daddy no more. Deal with it. 6 foot 4 and they dropped him. Plopped. Mopped him up. And you be next maybe. Shrinks and dinks. Talk till you're blue in the face. Daddy be dead, Mommy be mad and you not safe no more. Mommy drinks. Let me be. Banshee, shrieking in the streets. I sweat. Hate. Clench. Wail. Always in that order.

Since he's lying on his stomach, just a part of his penis is showing. As I suspected, it cannot be hard. But what am I doing here? Almost fully clothed on top of a man who won't look at me. I take it in my mouth.

The fire of grief welds you into someone new. When you're bent over, bone thin, so empty you have to stand up in stages to give the skin time to cover the body, that changes you. I have more in common with little old ladies than with my girlfriends. Men bore me easily, their lives so simple next to mine. Having been bathed in scalding fear, I am now afraid of nothing. I don't belong in this world anymore.

I lick this man's ass.

People like to talk about time. It takes time, Kathy, time. Time, the great healer. Time, it heals all wounds. Time! Time! Time! Well, time has its limits, my friends. Time may diminish, but it does not restore. If you rely solely on time, you may not feel the abject pain anymore, but neither are you fully alive.

I lick inside. I find it wonderful.

And time can be the enemy too. Take this man here, his penis half erect. My grief gets better with time, his only gets worse. Every day something else is taken away. Time is both his greatest wish and his greatest curse.

He's coming. Nothing's impossible…yet.

Every morning, he tells me, he must fall out of bed and lie on the floor, waiting for the meds to kick in. Only then can he move enough to stand up and start his day. If I am older than my years, this young man is ancient.

I press my breasts against him. We will never do this again and I'll never know what it meant to him. I give him one last kiss and look directly into his eyes. But it's too much for me. It's time for the Angel of Life to fly away.

robin burrows

QUALITY

She was in the shower when he rang, bundling her wet hair,
slipping into a thick robe and opening the door.
They are both surprised at her effect on him.

Brad, from Quality Stone.
He is average looking, average build, average job, she thinks,
      but really doesn't know. She never works.
She steps back opening the door.
He comes in to examine the stained marble entry.

Weeks go by.
One night, she thinks of him while pulling down the sheets:

he had gasped, almost, frozen a little,
his eyes soft and embarrassed.
She had taken his breath away.

SPENT

Last year spent alone in a small town
looking for someone
on this side of the screen door.
I have defeated myself. How can I talk about it?
Needing too much, it's better I stay in again.

He spoke and it became uneasy.
He had believed he could.
She believed, too.
I'll tell you one thing I have learned,
I will tell you the thing I have learned:
one day it ends.
There isn't time for this distance.
Can't you put down your fork and press me into the chair?
Surely, he doesn't want my creepy back-porch desire, well what am I to do?
I didn't care for lunch.

I write about a man who became a ghost.
My very alive sister keeps turning up dead as I write;
disturbing, since we are close
and her health isn't good, but dead,
all for a poem that still fails.
And what poem do you want to write?
The one where not a watermelon seed goes wasted;
every last look, every light true.
One I will not regret.

THE RED HILLS

I arrived in Chama with a spooky roan mare and two dogs that were my shadows. I wanted to learn about clay. I wanted to see her work firsthand. She was called Lucia, had red hair she dyed orange and too delicate for the winds. She lived here anyway. This land of crones holds onto a woman and carves her.

Clint was wild as the blowing dirt. He said he was no one's and that only his painting could reach out, which seemed to honestly sadden him. One night he saw me in *El Faroll* so we danced a few. My boots were laced as tight as I felt. How could I ever make the earth speak in my hands like she did?

Did I want to see his studio, he asked. I did, and he took me seven blocks down to his adobe. Starting with those boots, I let him work everything off, until I stood naked in the cold in front of a white hanging canvas. He brought me up against it, took an orange tube of oils and made her hair all around us. His fingers looked thin as her neck yesterday when she hung it and cried again about the Hopi atop her horse, a sorrel beauty.

Lucia, I told her, you should drive away, see Vancouver like you said.

Then there was the morning she bent over me, sweating, and I thought she was about to kiss me. She did and it didn't surprise me, it was a place for her fear while her fine black bowls fired in the kiln. We took a shower and didn't get dressed. The monsoon was roughing up the sky, mini-blinds slapping above our shoulders and the room smelled of electricity and Dial soap.

We heard him wipe his feet. Through the screen door Clint's eyes fell on us, lay like welts on her body on the nappy couch. Lucia, her mouth so red, like the blood in my cheeks. We didn't move until he swung in like he was starved and said it seemed sure he could fix her transmission. It was a '66 Corvette and all at once the whole desert soaked up the rain.

There he stood staring down, her man worn as a salesman. In just that instant, the way it does, the world changed. I felt all my need and my heart dropped like a white iris on black velvet. For that strong moment leading into months, I was in love and that's how it all began. When I pulled the clay through my fingers, it breathed into itself, and I took long rides into the red northern hills just looking at the shape of things.

SECOND CHANCE

I'm framed by two x-rays on the wall,
then and now.
I've been given second chances.
I know I'm lucky to have a leg.
In the beginning, I couldn't wait to see pictures of my fractures,
my hands rubbing the film where it hurts and for proof—
the dark gashes must grow white as china, as clean
     sheep carcass in the wet spring Uintas.
     I would run those dirt roads, my sister and I running ten thousand feet
     above everything.
     Her illness catching up, her heart, her baby girl with the open spot
     where angels whisper.
     Today, I won't look.

This is what I can expect now,
     Dr. Rumack says, hands in the pockets of his white coat,
but I'm a dancer, gams they called 'em,
fumbling for a Kleenex which I will use on the walk to the car,
sadder than anyone who hasn't known bad luck.
Shards, metal bolts, the fine shin hollowed by a rod, starting it up
again in a dry sun,
     a leg feels wooden without hope.

Tonight at the barn, I put my cheek to horse muzzle and take in
     the fresh timothy grass breathing,
 run my hand over the withers that crushed me when we lost footing on the slope
     rain, a bobcat, lush under foot, a deer jumped.
The quality of life, the exquisite quality.
I put my mouth over a velvet nostril and inhale.

There was a man who called me Rosebud,
     he would throw his life away.
I buried him
and stood by a fire holding on and drinking down what he had not finished
leaving his body and bones.

craig bergman
MY FRST WIFE

We first met at the coroner's. I love telling people that I met my wife at the coroner's. But the best part is why I was there—to claim the body of my first wife. I was at work, closing a very important deal with Redco Insurance, when my assistant came frantic into my office. I knew someone had died because she knows better than to interrupt me while I'm on the phone with big clients.

"Frank?"

There was an intimacy in her voice. Her tone slid down. I figured something had happened to one of my parents.

"It's your wife. They need to speak with you at the hospital. They said they could only speak with next of kin. I told them you were in an important meeting, but they wouldn't listen."

She stood there wearing that cashmere sweater I bought her for Secretary's Day. Her breasts swelling with sadness. Am I checking out my secretary's breasts while my wife could be lying dead in a hospital? Yes. And sad to say, I was hoping the news was bad because, honestly, I always liked this secretary.

FAT HIPPY BABIES

The fan is blowing loudly against the wall. A young hippie couple sits on a maroon couch talking about life. The coffee guy leans against the counter, hitting on the waitress. Outside, the LA streets dry off after two days of pummeling rain. The sky is clear and twinkling with stars. The storm has left for now. I grow despondent when the skies are gray and puffy with clouds. I start to think about all the things that are missing in my life, all of the things I should have done, said, thought. My mind is muddled, riddled with puddles, making it difficult to write without soaking my shoes through. The smudges of thought make completing a task impossible. Conversations are stilted, emotions watery and leaking. But the heavens are quiet now; the thunderclaps are memories. Pretty blonde girls take back the streets and traffic flows at a comfortable pace. The movie theaters are piling with viewers and the bougainvilleas are smiling. As for me, I'm good. I'm calm. I'm at one again, one again, with the pulse of the air, the prince of the City of Angels flowing with the workers, struggling actresses, machine-gun operators, parking validators. I'm one with the heavens, living side by side with the dead, unaware of the bad memories that have haunted my thoughts for so long. I'm another happy writer, red-inked pen in hand, making whoopee with the page, silently hoping the hippie couple will get married and have fat babies and live forever.

THE LIFE PLANNED OUT, PART I

This is the last poem I will ever write. I'm hanging up my pen and getting married. Married! Can you believe it? I never thought the day would come when I'd find someone crazy enough to share a bed with me for eternity. Someone to listen to me complain and cry and whine and belch and kvetch. But I did, and she's not half bad looking, actually. In fact, she's hot. I know, I'm in shock. She loves me, doody diapers and all. And she wants to live with me and drink my cum and make babies. It's all rather romantic. She owns a little plot of land down South, in Georgia to be exact. Yeah, she's a farmer. She grows organic dandelions and sells them to expensive tea makers around the world. I'm going to learn the business and help her do everything from planting to harvesting to selling. Yep, we'll be happy and grow old and fat together. And when I die, my kids will bury me out back beneath this old juniper tree that's been there since the Civil War. Finally, I know where I'm headed in life. And I won't be needing this writing thing anymore. I really only started with it in the first place because I was a miserable bastard and horny. But that's history. I'm putting down the pen and picking up a hoe. I'll be seeing you.

THE LIFE PLANNED OUT, PART II

Shit. You're not gonna believe this. I'm back. Yeah, I know, it was too good to be true. We broke up. She said she couldn't see us making it in the long haul, that I was too needy. I'm devastated. I cried for two weeks straight. I'm still crying as I write this. I had to get pills from my psychiatrist friend to keep me from taking an overdose. I'm miserable. Suddenly the skies are gray again and it's as if I've not changed one bit. If anything, I've regressed and am worse off than before. I don't know where to look for love now. I just don't know how. Oh, girl. All my friends call me a fool for thinking it would work out. What am I gonna do now? I had to pull all my notebooks out of the garbage and set up my writing desk again. I'm so embarrassed to pass fellow writers at poetry readings. I feel their snickers, their derisive glances burning holes in my old beat up jean jacket, which I also retrieved from the refuse bin. Along with my horn rimmed glasses and my crumpled cap. It's another endless cycle of masturbation, coffee, late night scribble sessions, high on morphine, codeine, vicadin, speed, whatever I can get my hands on. I am gonna miss the normal life, the life planned out and orderly, like so many rows of dandelions. Oh darling, you've ruined me, just ruined me. Where will they bury my dead body when I'm done? Who will care for my debilitated mind as I grow weary? Oh, Georgia, you are just an old sweet song.

STARTING OVER TIME

I'm lying on the carpeting in Marisa's hotel room at the Avalon. The cell phone is sitting open on my notebook and the commodore is at the window. The light from the cell helps me see in this darkened room. It is 5.54 am, Wednesday, and I'm awake after a difficult dream. Marisa walked away from me, she left me, and I was furious. I woke up and spent forty minutes writing it down. The old man was there, pointing fingers, and it frightened me. But I am better now, spread out, listening to the early shifting. Hotel workers chat outside our room. Marisa is turning over in her sleep and I'm thinking of walking to Starbucks for a doppio Macchiato. It helps me shit and I need help this morning. I can't shit and I can't write a single interesting word. The pillow is soft under my chin, though, and I love this time of day. The starting over time. A bus drives down Olympic and Marisa breathes soft like a baby. I wonder what she's dreaming about. I wonder what she'll say when she wakes, not finding me there beside her.

INFINITE MECHANISMS

One day I'll tell you of all the miracles I've experienced.
I'll tell of the near fatal collisions
And the missed bad opportunities.
I'll tell of the birth of my nephews when simple science said no.
I'll tell of the miracle of vision,
Of watching my lover floss in the shadow of the cupboard,
Of the way her nipples turn inward when she's at rest,
I'll tell of the sight of my mother walking towards me
Embracing me in her love,
A love that doesn't question or see-saw,
A love that fixes me when I'm broke.

People, people, people,
I'll tell of the miracle of sound
As when Miles Davis plays on the public radio station
And my mind is relieved of its burdens.
I'll tell of the miracle of breath,
Of organ function,
Of infinite mechanisms operating in unison
Following only the one voice.

Miracles, miracles, miracles,
Feed me a steady diet of these wonderful moments when
What seems hopeless fills with sudden light.
The times when I've asked the unseen to save me.
The miracle that someone is really listening,
The miracle of patience
When Marisa loves me and loves me and
Gives me all of what she has
And I sit here and look at what I don't get
Which is my curse.

Oh, dreaded curse,
Turn away.
Flip to your blessed side.
Allow this Light to give me everything I need:
The creativity, the mode of expression, the power to do,
The miracle of remembering,
Remembering me.

leda rogers

BROOKLYN
[excerpt]

"Can I help you, young man?"

"Yeah, I would like a ticket to see this here movie, please."

"It's like, in Italian with subtitles, man, real cool."

"What does sub-titles mean?"

"It means, man, that the English words, dig it, are written on the screen, get this man, so you can understand what they are talking about, now this is crazy, kid, if you don't speak Italian, right. Like, do you speak Italian?"

"No, I speak American."

"Like you mean English, kiddo. Well then, you'll have to read the subtitles, won't you? Can you dig it man?"

"What kind of language are you speaking?"

"Hey man, like it's English, dig it? Oh, you mean the dig it's and crazy man's, like that?"

"Yeah…man?"

"Hey, now you're talking beat, man. You're a real Beatnik now. Can you dig it?"

"I think so. Crazy…man?"

"Cool, you dig it, man, real cool, man, real cool! So do you want a ticket to this like, cool flick, with subtitles. Did I mention it was in Italian, man?"

I'm standin' there with my hands in the pockets of my Dungarees. By now I have to go to the bathroom so's I'm shiftin' from one foot to the other. I'm shakin' 'cause it's cold outside and this guy is starin' down at me from the ticket window. I can see the fog that his breath is making on the window, while he's talkin' with me. It looks like frost on a winter's day when it snows. He's got big lips, cherry red and black eyes. Every once in a while he takes out some bills from underneath where he's standin' and puts them in order, turning each bill so's they're all facin' the same way.

"Uh, like it sounds cool, but I ain't much on readin', man. You dig it? But hey, ya' know, like I really have to take a wiz, otherwise I'm gonna, like, pee in my pants. You can dig that, huh? Do ya' think, like, maybe I could go in for a minute to use the men's room, man? Would that be cool?"

"Like, how would I know you wouldn't stay in there and watch the movie? You know people give me that line all the time."

"Well, you know me! And I swear I'll be right back and talk with ya' some more. Please, mister, I really gotta go. Besides, I don't speak Italian and I can't read. Cool man, huh?"

I'm crossin' my legs at this point and I don't even know if I could make it to the God damned bathroom. I watch him as he turns the 'OPEN' sign around. It reads, 'BE BACK IN TEN MINUTES.' He opens a little door on the side of the booth and pokes his head out, then he sets one long leg out while holding on to the side of the doorway. Then out comes his other leg. He stands up, turns around and locks the door. Boy, is he tall. He must be 7 feet tall. He grabs my hand and pulls me toward the entrance of the theater. My Ma' used to do that when I was a kid. If we were shoppin' in a department store and I had to pee, she would grab my hand and drag me to the nearest bathroom. It was always the Ladies Room and I'd have to go in a stall with her so's I could pee. She would pull down my pants, angry-like, and say, "Pee," and she'd watch while I'd pee. Then she would shake my dick to make sure there was no more and pull my pants back on. Then drag me out and yell, "That's the last time! Next time you pee in your pants!"

"Here's the Men's Room. Go in and do what you have to do and make it quick."

I walk into the bathroom. It stinks in there. The white paint is all gray and peeling off the walls. The sink is rusty from where the water leaks. I go into one of the stalls. It has no door on it. Neither did the other one so I have no choice. There is a hole in the wall between the two stalls. If someone were in the other one, they could watch me peein'. Like my Ma' used to do. She'd watch me pee all the time. She'd open the door and come right in the bathroom like it was nothin', pretendin' not to notice. But I would catch her eye glancin' down at my dick, tryin' to get a real good look. I pee real quick and get out of there.

"Did you wash your hands?"

"Yeah."

I lied. I always wash my hands after I go to the bathroom, but I just wanted to get out of there. It gave me the creeps.

He grabs my hand again and takes me outside and back to his booth. He opens the lock with his long bony fingers and gets back into the booth the same way he got out. First one leg and arm, then his head, then the second leg and arm, and shut the door. I hear him lock it from inside. Then he counts the money. I guess he wants to make sure it's all there. I don't see how anyone could have taken it while we went to the bathroom. He's kinda weird.

"Well thanks a lot, mister, for lettin' me use the bathroom. I guess I'll be goin' now... man."

"Oh sure, man, like you do something nice for someone and then they split on you. Fine, like split, it's cool with me, creep."

"I didn't think you'd want me hangin' around, that's all."

"Hey, like, dude, you're cool. I like your rap. Anyway, I thought, well, I get off soon and maybe, well, man, it's just an idea. But you see I play this gig over on 7th Avenue and I thought I could drag you along."

"Like you did to the bathroom?"

"Cute. No, I mean maybe you'd like to hear me do some sticks on sticks. Man, I play drums."

"The drums? You play the drums? Wow! I can't believe it! Holy cow, you play the drums? Man!"

"Cool, huh?"

"Cool? I've been wantin' to play the drums forever. It's been my secret wish! Oh man, you ain't kiddin' me, are ya'? For real?"

"Like, for real, man, real. Cool, kid, keep your cool, now. This is a sophisticated place, a jazz club. Now they don't let no kids like you in there, but you're with me, dig it. So don't say nothing. Keep your cool. Listen, I got like forty-five minutes left on my shift, man, dig it? So, like, how would you like to sneak into the movies, man? Just walk through those double doors and find a seat and watch the movie 'til I come and get you. Then we'll go to the club. Are you cool with that?"

"Yeah, man! But what if I can't understand it?"

"It doesn't need a big explanation. Go with your feelings."

melinda mcgraw

BLUE

"I love you so much," he says and he kisses me tender, and I respond as best I can. We are making love and he is over me and on me and in me, and I do what I've been doing for months. I tolerate it and try to stay calm, breathing away the waves of panic that want to grip me. Soon, it is too much and—

"Sorry, I can't." Stumbling to the bathroom. Suddenly gurgling. Awash.

He comes in. "Honey, what is it? What, why are you so sad?"

My body is racked with bottomless sobs, the kind usually reserved for after funerals, and I try not to find the words. His brown, perfect hand rests on my knobby knee. It is strong and smooth. His other is around my hip. I am perched on the toilet and he kneels in front of me, face upturned.

He is the most beautiful man that I have ever known or ever seen. Heavy brows over chocolate ocean eyes, fat lips that were made for love, small perfectly crooked teeth. His shoulders are blue from the pool light outside spilling onto the tiles of the bathroom floor. A lovely ghost, he smells of coffee and basil. The hum of the bedroom fan calls us back to bed, but I am inert and broken on the commode, full of longing and sorrow and jagged guilt. Because this man has stayed. He has saved me from myself. He has never tricked me. He is more giving than I will ever be and more than I deserve—but still I need to get away, to shake him off. I am invaded by his tenderness and strangled by his guileless, musical love.

"I just need it to be like it was in the beginning. Before you loved me so much."

"I know you do," he says, always so brave, and he cradles my face in his hands.

This is my husband.

This is my marriage.

ellen kimmel

GENEROSITY

I'm at the Biltmore Hotel downtown,
but I already told you that in another poem.
Zev Yaroslavsky just gave a speech about
homelessness in L.A. He told the story
he's probably told a thousand times about his daughter,
how she sat down next to a homeless man
on a bench and talked to him for twenty minutes.
Then when they finished their conversation,
she reached into her bag to get a few bucks to give him, and
when she stretched out her hand, he refused to accept the money.
He said what she gave him was more valuable than money.
"And what did she give him?" Zev asked rhetorically.
She looked him in the eye. She saw him. He wasn't invisible
as the two of them were to all the people who walked by them that day.
Pulling out of valet parking onto Grand Street,
a homeless man walked right past my car
and didn't see me. Driving to work this morning,
the homeless man on the bicycle with his
life's belongings in the crate attached to the back
was stopped at the stop sign when I approached.
He waved me to go ahead and make my left turn.
I waved him to go first.
He nodded for me to go.
It went on like this for, I'd say, about five minutes,
neither one of us wanting to go before the other.
So there we were, Friday morning at 8am,
at the corner of Martel and Clinton,
not just looking each other in the eye,
but smiling and laughing at the ridiculousness of our generosity.
Without taking there can be no giving.

FUN FACTS

Every morning posted in the elevator at my apartment complex
is a new flyer with the weather forecast for the day and
a few fun facts to contemplate while riding down to the parking lot.

This morning I learned that there are 6800 different languages in the world and every two
weeks one language becomes extinct. And that
Mona Lisa has no eyebrows, but during her time, it was a sign
of beauty for a woman to shave her eyebrows.

The Latina girls I work with get in trouble with their probation officers
if they shave their eyebrows, because it's a sign of gang involvement, which is a violation of
the conditions of their probation.

Did you know that the dot that appears over the letter *i* is called a *tittle*?
Bob didn't know that, but he knew about Da Vinci's painting.
The expression *tying the knot* comes from an old Roman custom where the bride's clothes
were tied up all in knots and the
groom was supposed to untie the knots.

My ex-husband didn't untie any knots on our wedding day.
He made knots, and then he made 23 years worth of knots—
knotty knots, fishing knots, double fisherman knots,
trucker's knots, square knots, water knots,
sailor's knots, diamond knots, loop knots.
Now, six months after the divorce,
I'm realizing he was trying to find the right knot.
The right knot holds under an extremely heavy load.

MANNA FROM HEAVEN

Vanita's brother fell out of a tree and died.
"What was he doing in a tree?" I asked
after expressing my condolences, because
it's not death etiquette to ask the question
we are all dying to ask first.
Vanita was sitting on the steps outside the school
contemplating life and thinking of going into a career in theology
because she wants to help people.
"He was picking bread fruit," she told me.
"What is bread fruit?" I asked.
She tried to explain what it looked like and tasted like—
big and roundish. She cupped her hands together
to show me the shape and size. It's not sweet.
It's more like a potato and you eat it with butter.
Since going to the Hollywood farmer's market
every Sunday morning, I thought I'd seen it all,
but I'd never heard of this Caribbean delicacy.
You have to pick it by hand.
You can't let it ripen and fall because
when it hits the ground, it splatters.
"It's like manna," Vanita told me.
"Manna?" I asked.
"That manna?" I asked again.
"Yes," she said, with faith in her eyes,
and for a moment I believed her.
There would be a miracle from heaven
to sustain me in my exile.

MY FATHER'S LIST

My father called me the other day to read me the list.
It was a list of things he thought would help me get through the divorce.
He keeps telling me to wait a year before I date because
that's what he heard from a radio psychologist in Florida.
I keep telling him okay, even though I already started dating,
and he knows I already started dating,
but he keeps telling me to wait a year.
That was number one on the list: Wait a year before dating.
Number two: Get a massage once a month.
Number three: Get a manicure and a pedicure once a month.
I didn't tell him I can't afford to do numbers two and three.
Number four: Don't talk to your Ex.
Number five: Don't talk to your Ex.
Number six: Go for the custody plan and financial settlement you want.
Number seven: Don't talk to your Ex.
Number eight: Swim every day.
Number nine: Go out with friends.
Number ten: Keep writing and keep throwing pots.
Ten years ago, even five, I would have dismissed my father's list, devalued it.
Now I think it's sweet. Now I see he loves me.

FALLING

I don't understand how I can fall so easily.

It's like I have a falling gene.

I keep trying to protect myself, but this thing is beyond me,

way beyond, and no matter how many times a day I tell myself,

or my friends tell me, not to fall, I keep falling.

It could be the sound of his laugh or the way he gets the words wrong –

like how he says *pontiphonicate*, instead of *pontificate*, or

it could be his soft touch on my elbow, or

how his fingers tickle my skin, or

how his body feels like it fits with mine when he's hugging me, or

how his voice gets all little boyish when he's telling me

the story about when he was four and his mother pulled him off the horse and

he didn't want to go, or it could be how he listens to music and

how he listens to me, his hand on my stomach as I speak.

His tenderness makes me feel my own.

His kindness makes me kind.

His love makes me loving.

I don't know why I was afraid of this for so long.

lucy mccusker

SMALL WORLD HOLLYWOOD

It's true.
I used to hang out in Hollywood.
That's right.
7 nights a week.
Melrose to the boulevard.
My salon was on Melrose.
We had an office space on the boulevard,
on the corner of Hollywood and Las Palmas.
We used that place for band members to crash,
to watch the Hollywood parades, X-mas, Halloween,
all of them.
To shoot dope, smoke dope, drink,
to smoke crack, drink,
pass out, get sick, get sick...
We did all of that.
It was pretty hardcore back then.
Somebody was always up in there doing something.
There were about fifteen offices on the top floor.
It was a real 30's style building.
All kinds of kooks renting places.
Artists, writers, dopers, rockers.

I met a girl in rehab out in Minnesota.
She had a space there, at the office building.
She said that she was a writer,
addicted to heroin.
She said that she almost never came out of her space.
Except to use the bathroom.
There were two bathrooms on either end of the building.
This girl stayed on the east side,

we were on the west.
I don't remember ever seeing her.

She told me she saw me once crossing Las Palmas
coming out of a bar.
She said I was wearing a black and white polka dot dress
with motorcycle boots.
She said I walked to the building and buzzed the intercom.
She said I waited a minute then
started kicking the security gate over and over
and over again.
She said she couldn't hear me, but could tell
I was yelling.
She said that a guy walked out with spiky hair dressed in all black.
She said that we put our arms around each other and walked
back across the street and into the bar.
Yea.
Small world Hollywood.
That was a small life.
Seems like a thousand lives ago.
It wasn't.
I heard that girl,
the writer addicted to heroin,
I heard that she died a year after rehab.
I heard that she never sold her second book.
I heard that she was back in Hollywood when it happened.

Yea.
Hollywood.
7 nights a week.

elizabeth bradley

BROKEN GLASS

Moroccan brass fills the cracks
in a stacked life of wants and wishes,
fucked up with broken glass—
every container a testament to a category
of the crazy rollercoaster thrill embarked upon
decades past.
Alcoholic imposter shattering
the postcard perfect fairy tale, cocky
character acting the part of affectionate spouse,
a six foot seven nightmare bear
coveting nonexistent cash and possessions,
no lottery here you stupid fuck. A lazy motherfucker
unwilling to work on anything
but his iconoclastic slackerhood and Saturday morning vodka,
hidden by colorful citric acid in a big fat plastic tumbler—
stashing the empty glass containers in
closets and corners,
freezers and cupboards,
too much of a big fat pussy to come clean and own
the fact he was a fuckup user
life destroyer.
Trading paychecks for maudlin art, statues, love beads,
and African masks—cultish and haunting
invoking terror in her own residence,
too scared to walk to the kitchen at midnight—
they might come alive wicked to feast,
bulging tongues flying off their pedestals—
don't fuck with freaky voodoo—
curses gods black magic have a way of pervading
like hardcore pornography ass fucking that won't escape

the playground of the unconscious,
symbolic of the demons floating in and out
of her consciousness—demons that led her to settle
for the distorted picture of domestic tranquility
escaping the incessant fucking and being fucked over
and under
and every which way while crystal skies rain shards of glass
through her heart
that just wanted to be loved, just wanted to be touched.
Glass reflecting images of fantasies long broken
and crumbled into piles of sand grains stuck
between her twenty toes and knotted hair,
teeth crunching and crumbling each last hope
into dust.

judeth oden

NASCENT

Two young men hunched over, I swear, like prep school boys in Exeter Hall, with one, I had to smile to myself, pouring over the dictionary—the dictionary! I swear Dimas was looking up the meaning of the word "ignoramus." He said he READ the word in a POEM. Eduardo's folded pieces of paper, poems and poems worth, covered the table, as he pushed the pen to a new, half-empty sheet, and my heart ached with pride. Pride feels a lot like anxiety. My chest gets tight and little wave of pain pushes up my torso stopping up my throat, cutting off oxygen to the brain, making my face red and fragmenting my sentences. Another little wave moves down my body to my stomach and all the acids slosh side to side.

Damn, my lips are chapped. And I haven't written for class. And I said I'd only stay an hour. Eduardo's writing about suffering and what it's like to watch someone die and the expression on the white man's face in a picture he saw where the white man was buying the land out from under Mexican feet. He writes about a room with white walls that's separating the brown from the black, and the brown and the black are fighting each other for the window high up along the ceiling. I ask him if he knows what "metaphor" means, or "symbolism." "No," he says, "What I'm trying to say is that the white walls are white people, like the cops, keeping blacks and Latinos separate. And the window, well, that's like what they're all fighting for. To be part of the wall. It's like gangs, how they kill each other. You see it all the time."

"Describe what the white man buying the Mexican's land looks like," I say. "He's got a wig on and one of those things, you know." Eduardo points to his throat, around his neck. "What's that called?" "A bow tie?" "Yeah, one of those."

We're sharing the office with Jeff. Jeff's taking over the class. I was just stopping by to give Eduardo his journal and to clean up some of the mess I'd left. But then Dimas showed me his poem and we talked about how it changed when he repeated the opening line in the middle and the end. And Eduardo wanted to read me another new poem. The boy's addicted. He writes seven at a sitting. And Jeff needed the office keys and the paper work. Jeff is on the phone with other students and potential students, telling them about the new class. His class. They're moving on from poetry to screenwriting. And we listen to his very strong and efficient voice asking for students by name. His English never gets stumped by their parents' Spanish. "Is Manuel there? Manuel. Manuel. Manuel. Yes, Manny."

"I've gotta go, guys. I have to go to MY writing class," I say. Dimas, I'm not kidding, is still reading the dictionary, muttering with his brows furrowed. Jeff joins our circle. He looks at the page. "Nascent," he says, "It's one of my favorite words. It means something is at the beginning. Like a nascent idea is just the beginning of an idea." "What does it mean to be at the end?" Dimas asks. "Nothing," says Jeff, "When an idea is at the end, it's not an idea anymore."

"Good question, Dimas."

I walk out with Eduardo. I bet he'll ask me for a ride. He lives in Lincoln Heights and I always get lost trying to find the freeway from over there. Henry's waiting in his new, very severely used, Honda, primer gray and real gray in spots. He's picking up his sister. "Where are you, now?" he asks. "Nowhere," I say, and he laughs at me. And by then Eduardo's down at the other end of the lot, walking past *El Pollo Loco*, all 4 feet 6 of him. He shouldn't be riding the bus after dark, I think. And my chest gets tight. And I get in my car, heading straight for the freeway.

leslie ward

SILK CHIFFON HEART

The vanilla musk moonlight shone through the open window, bathing my face in white magic as I lay in my bed on the second floor in the house of my childhood on a sweltering July night of my seventeenth year. The distant ringing of a telephone cut through the fog of my teenage creamsicle dreams, and his voice, like torn velvet, floated through the receiver, grasping and reaching through the cobwebs in my head.

"Meet me," he said, "Meet me outside in 10 minutes. I'll pick you up. I want to see you."

I opened my mouth to speak. The alkaline hiss of the summer night becoming louder in my ears, as I struggled to find my voice through the cacophony in my head.

"It's 1:00am!" I whispered, not wanting to wake my parents who were sleeping across the hall in our beautiful home on the right street in the right neighborhood, filled with golden opportunity and dismal, soul-crushing silence.

"Please, just meet me. We can go to the beach house for a while."

Confusion, dread and desire fused with the purple-black ache of teenage longing, and it was too much for me.

"Okay…okay," I replied quietly, knowing what was to come, knowing that my silk chiffon heart was not ready for the bias cut satin beauty of the varsity boy in the white Toyota Celica, knowing that I would abandon myself while searching for my reflection in the fun house mirrors of his half-moon, black-silk wishing well eyes.

I dressed in silence. With my heart in my throat, I inched my way down the newly carpeted spiral staircase, praying to my weary, tattered angels for a sign, a redemptive, choir-in-the-rafters moment. As I traveled down the stairs, down from the safety of my room, down from the altar of goodness, down from my verdant, nougatine youth, I looked up to see my adolescence smiling at me from the family photos on the wall. My clear, starlight eyes and perfect smile betraying the insecurity and restlessness that inhabited every inch of my cheerleader persona. I tiptoed through the silent kitchen, pausing for a moment to gaze through the window at the moon that called me out with its siren's song, fever-kiss promises of love. I stepped out the back door, and closing it carefully behind me, took a deep breath and ran into the night.

THE NOTHING INSIDE ME

I am tired of hearing myself talk about my lonely marriage
and my crazy job and oh, poor me.
I am tired of running from place to place like a lunatic.
I am tired of trying to keep all the plates spinning.
I am tired of hoping he will again someday
find me attractive and sexy and clever.

I don't know if I'll be married this time next year.
I don't know if I'll have anything intelligent to say, ever again.
I want to know how long a person can go without affection
before they go completely insane.

I want to know
why the dishwasher is making that strange noise,
how my jeans ended up in Henry's closet,
why the television is on,
why no one has thrown out the rotten fruit.

I want to know
what my horoscope says today, why I can't remember if I paid the water bill,
why I ate that Ho-Ho.
Where the hell is Pacoima?
Is this thing on?
Is that it?
Is that all I've got?

teri goldman
LIMITATIONS

The tall, dark-haired stranger
crosses the street in front of the car.
He wears black pants, black loafers, and a black shirt,
the top two buttons left open to reveal tan skin.
The man walks with a slight limp,
indiscernible until his third step, sometimes his fourth.
He takes a puff of his cigarette and wobbles.
The air exits his mouth
and two normal steps follow.
His stare lingers in the air like haunted beauty,
a rock star gliding across a smoky stage:
slide, slide, slide, plunk,
slide, slide, plunk.

Down the block,
a leopard-spotted cat waits
behind the bushes in pounce position,
back legs raised,
front legs hunched,
nose pointing forward toward potential prey.
A temperate breeze kicks up from the west,
and the cat stills, ears twitching,
eyes scanning the grass line,
the impending Serengeti sandstorm
beckoning it to run for cover.

Instinct taunts the reality of a six-pound existence
as the little lion prepares for attack.
But the cat deems the limping man too large for the take.
Still, it squats lower and lower,

watching through whispering leaves,
smelling fire and musk,
channeling its evolutionary heritage.

I understand the deliverance of destiny from birth:
a wounded walk,
a hunter's instinct.
I have longed to stalk life with the confidence of the kill,
to saunter in grace without the dread of missteps;
but I was born with sensitive feet
and loved ones who remind me of my smallness.

laurel benton

THE ONLY THING

today was hell.
it's a cold hard world,
and i can't find a home for this kitty.
there have been signs up
in the neighborhood saying
that someone has been killing cats with a machete.
it's a beautiful day in the neighborhood...
life was a nicer place not so long ago,
and if i do stretch pose,
i might not get turkey neck.
on the big wedding card, my sister wrote,
"great blessings to you both,
i hope that your future together
will be full of all the joy and magic that life can...potato."
i wish i could salsa dance, but
the only thing i do efficiently is fuck up.

linda mcmillin pyle
ICE PICK

When Tracy put her ice pick into my neck,
when she pressed her elbows into my spine,
I remembered the gravestones,
the crematorium with the twirling metal exhaust fan that alerted us
to the burning inside.

When I think of the cold
marble mausoleum,
its columns and Greek revival architecture,
its gray face, its fearsome drawers and corpses,
I cringe.

How the hell has Forest Lawn Memorial
gotten stuck in the back of my head?
I was in my brown wool jacket and blue snow pants sailing down the hill below the mauso-
leum on a saucer and,
CRACK, I hit the ice of the snow-covered pond.
I hit my tailbone hard.
I don't remember if I cried.
Jeez, that was 40 some years ago.
How can I still feel the saucer crack as it went over the bank?
Now I got this ghoulish cemetery stuck where my
head joins my neck.

I guess that's what happens when you grow up across the street from a cemetery.
It becomes your playground.
Once, we were sledding down another hill deeper into the graveyard
and smacked into a gravestone.
Bad luck, we said.

One late night, while walking home through the graveyard, my brother told my sister and me that he just heard Ed Gein had escaped the mental hospital.
He was on the loose in Forest Lawn.
We ran like hell.
Ed was the inspiration for *Silence of the Lambs*.

Hey, if it was Anthony Hopkins running behind me now and looking for someone to make a lampshade out of, I might not have been so scared.
Later, I learned to drive in the cemetery.
No worries about killing anyone there.

After I moved away,
I used to dream about it.
I used to wander there at night in nightmares.
I used to see skulls with burning red eyes at the locked gate.

Who can tell me now?
Who can hold my hand and walk me through the Valley of Death now that Grandpa is dead and they didn't let me go to the funeral?
Who can tell me how to mourn him?
How do I stop being afraid?
How do I stop having headaches and how do I not fear the ice pond ?
Who could slip on four-inch thick glaciers?
Who could be white-haired fright wig over an oven and red flaming orbiting eyes?

If the ashes are hot,
then why is death so frozen and breathless?
Why is life so merry and summer grass?
Why is winter the ice palace in my neck,
the meat locker between my neck and head scarf?

I mean, hey, I'm grown now.
What kind of imbecile would be afraid of that!
Jeez, Marge, I know it's colder than hell in Minnesota, but freezing a block of fear in there, fear of a cemetery,

for Christ sake, of all things.
Can you beat that?
I am sorry Grandpa had to die of liver cancer.
I didn't mourn him.
I froze him in a dream.

I loved Grandpa's garden.
He lived with us.
When I came home from school, I had to ask if it was okay to turn on the TV.
Grandpa was resting, dying on the sagging couch.
He always said yes.

He wouldn't want me to be in grief,
splayed out on my orange saucer on the hard ice.
I see the pond below the mausoleum now in summer, with the mallard ducks swimming and
the green grass on the hill once covered in snow.

Grandpa picked up the pieces for Grandma when her husband,
one of his ten brothers, died suddenly of a stroke and left her with
four small children to raise.
He married her after a proper time had expired and grew corn and tomatoes
and raised baby chicks
and us.

I remember his face,
his olive sun-tanned skin our family calls *the Austrian hide*.
I remember the tang of freshly-picked raspberries still warm from the sun
offered to us in his hand

Grandpa,
put the ice pick in deep.
Land the blows hard.
Soften my neck with your kindness.
Let me go to the freezer and find
the fear has evaporated
like dry ice.

katy melody
REVIEW

It's the inside of my head,
the inside of my head,
the film
of people passing,
overdue letters to write,
my niece who needs comfort,
the piles
everywhere,
bills and catalogues,
taxes and photos,
financial plans.
The letters mix up,
like Scrabble pieces
and I can't even say it.
Loose beads and keys,
clothing stacked and waiting
for hems and darning,
hair clumped in corners,
books piled next to the bed,
recyclables waiting to be sorted
and all I want is sleep.
But the horn keeps blaring
this friend to call,
this plant to pot,
this sill to paint.
The letters fall off of my fingers
like confetti,
and I can't find the words
to clear the surfaces,
shine the floors,
seal envelopes and

fates of every Hummel and book
waiting for dusting.
And sleep is sent to the end of the line
that winds back through every year I see,
when I lay me down to
try and shut out
the rapacious review,
the hungry dogs,
barking and whining loud,
so the neighbors can hear,
can know I'm still not catching up,
can know I'm still running
from the hounding reminders
of all that threatens to unravel.
So sleep,
the thought that I could be left to dream,
is thrown down as my indulgence,
my sin against the state of everything
I haven't done.

REVELATIONS

I lie across you,
my humpback whale
time has no course here.
We are only riding waves
of some other horizon,
one we have yet to speak,
calling back a time before edges,
the geometry of the known.
We curve together,
carving centuries of water.
I am climbing the steps of your ladder,
your walls fall open like a parting sea,
revealing bones and purple eddies.
I take your hand before diving
(birds watch from the bank and
wash themselves in our wake),
I swim down
inside your silence,
guided by turtles and instinct
love floats by like seahorses,
dancing and puffing,
clouds shadow our turnings
and I let you go.
In the kelp forest there are no markers
but the sun's light falls here
and I swim up to meet it,
feel your pulse in mine,
as I stroke and kick the surface.

LICORICE DREAM

I'm here
behind the trees,
the forest is dark
but you will venture in
to touch my bark
minding rivulets and gullies,
sidetracks.
I'm only wondering what you would say
if you had—
but time is not the healer,
don't you one bit believe it.
We're all here for seduction.
The green and the dark habits
lying in wait.
Keep walking
to the smell of it,
the scratch against your cheek,
the blood you can lick—
it's all initiation.
I wouldn't lie,
blow you feathers,
but this you can hold onto:
the licorice of night to meet you
and no one is coming.
It's dreaming gets you this,
this wolf at your splintered door.

COMMUNION

We're standing in these spaces,
looking up,
our faces feel the breeze pass over,
traces left behind,
like leaves,
dead and crackling underfoot,
it's a time for mourning,
then for walking on,
this sky will find another day
and so will I,
the wind moves us all along,
before we know,
it's better that way.

chris shearer

BLACK SHAPES

I couldn't get to sleep last night. I breathed deep into my belly, but the night would not dissolve into distance, the darkness would not loosen its grip on my banging heart, and I turned out onto the highway where my life was most open-ended. I stood there with my thumb out, the grass dusty and winded, sparkling with soot and litter, the asphalt shoulder spotted with the crushed dried carcasses of unlucky raccoons, woodchucks, possums, owls, falcons, skunks, and even porcupines. In this howling sweep, great square trucks rush past, sucking the refuse behind them and shaking the concrete slabs like they were being pounded by piledrivers. High up in the cabs of these behemoths sit wild bloodshot eyed, bandy-legged truckers, pupils dilated with truck-stop amphetamines, t-shirts grimy with days of road sweat and speed residue and coffee fumes. Once in a blue moon one would slam to a stop, trailer screeching in protest, and I would pull myself up to the big seat on the chrome handrail that would grow sweaty under my grip when the cab yanked back and forth, whipped by the weight of the loaded trailer skidding on the snow and ice packed highway in the dead of winter. "Hold on!" he would scream, "This is it!" and then suddenly, miraculously, the Jake-brake would straighten out the rig, and we'd be cutting the night again, lights gleaming on the dashboard, shapes rumbling black past the big flat windows. Dog-tired, I'd try to sleep again, only to be wakened by another hellish near-death careen into the night. But anything was better than my toes turning to frozen clay inside my leather boots outside on the road, or wandering the coffee shop sunglass racks with my brain screaming for sleep and only willpower holding me up for hour after crawling hour, sustained by the knowledge that the cyclical nature of luck would give me a great gift of fortune on the next day equal in amplitude to the shitstorm of the night before—a good long ride with an ex-Air Force surgeon who would tell me about the old man's arteries found in autopsied twenty year old pilots, old, he believed, from salt and junk-food and too much stress. Old before their time, bodies tearing through a decade for every year of piloting jets at speeds and g-forces that centrifuge the inner cage into bands of like-bodied elements, glistening in the parlance of too much excitement and then separate from the symmetry that kept them moist, calcifying and hardening, creaking and calling for some light wind to rustle the tops of wheat. Or a redneck pitbull breeder with a black goatee and hippie hat who would tell me that sometimes, although he was not proud of it, he would cut the paws off of a bitch that he suspected of having no heart for fighting, and throw the dying animal into the ring to see if she would fight as she bled to death, so that he would know if her pups had the bloodlines to be champion fighters. You can learn a lot on the road. You can learn about the imminent race war between black and white that every sane white man is stockpiling arms for in the backwoods, and that weight training builds muscles which, if not maintained, turn to yellow fat, and that sometimes men with their penises shot off in the war like to watch their wives fuck other men, and that some fist fighters are helpless when they are forced to wrestle on the ground. Once, made crazy by the grinding cycle of luck, I stepped off and crossed through the fence into a freight-train yard and learned of another cycle, one that governs the tramps that ride the rails from Lincoln, Nebraska, to the apple orchards of Washington, past the weirs of the Tillamook on the Deschutes, where broken, blue-maned men talk of river-washed girls that disappeared, or were taken away, or became spirits. I learned, on the trains, that you can always get a job in Lincoln, that the mosquitoes in Oroville will eat you alive, and that day-old tomato sauce congealed on the lid of a tin can can kill you. I learned that Union Pacific polices their trains with a Nazi diligence, but Sante Fe will let you ride unmolested. I learned that sleeping in the cab of an unlocked piggy-back Ford Ranger chained to the top of a flatcar is nearly impossible, the soft seat and truck suspension only amplifying the constant clack-clack-clack of the bouncing flatcar. And I learned that some men, for whatever reason, will die if they stop moving for more than a few days in a row, and that no amount of liquor or free dumpster turkey or down pillows can stop the flailing that's inside them, and that I am not one of those men, except at night, when I can't see a thing, and all that is left are the shapes rumbling black past the banging of my heart.

justin klippel

DRIFTER

I pick a card out of the deck.
I don't really care what color or suit it is.
I keep it in my coat pocket
just for tonight,
then it will slam the door.
I'm a drifter
when it comes to love
because I only get turned on by whores.
They're beautiful
because they know who they are
and they take me as I am
without questions.

UNHONORABLE DISCHARGE

They seem so nice
that I just might soil them.
This one goes out to all those sweet ladies.
Maybe they don't love me because I never owned a dog.
Every guy owns a dog at one point in his life.
Caring for another in that way wasn't a household fixture.
There was this advice:
"When all else fails, pull her pants down."
Maybe that's why I am not honorable,
why I am comfortable with one night stands,
no strings attached,
just fish swimming in the cold water of my tank.

THE DETAIL

The small patch of hair
is growing on her tailbone.
It's not an imperfection

and when she wears her low-cut tops,
it's a window for me to see through
her expensive clothes,
her sweet smell,
and her just-enough makeup.
Many girls have tattoos in this area,
but a small patch of hair
pulls the lever on my slot machine.

CHAIN LINKED

The smoke of my cigarette
is slowly escaping my mouth.
My eyes keep watch over me
from the mirror.
My pen is going back and forth
between my fingers.
The pen is attached to a chain on the desk.
In all of the air on Earth one thing lies—
its creativity.
I try to catch it with a green fish tank net.
Microscopic and a behemoth,
waiting to be caught,
when missed it dangles off my desk
swinging back and forth.

DEMENTIA

From outside
I tighten the screws to the window.
This screwdriver has been used often
to puncture repeatedly
through a square piece of wax paper.
No matter how many holes are exposed,
the paper stays intact.
When put up against the window,
through the holes
I can see the rusty cane
lying next to the bed.
The sound of the fishpond attracts the birds.
I go into the clear roof shed to get the birdseed.
I fill the birdhouse with a big scoop.
Looking through the holes again,
I see the dust marks on her side of the bed.

LOUDER

My body aches
just after a concert
from slamming in the pit.
It's a good kind of soreness,
the way a boxer must feel after a victory.
The bed in my room is softer,
food hits a certain taste bud that wasn't there before,
the cigarette smoke seems deserved.
A telephone rings in my ears for two days,
compliments of the band,
and the turning of the pages in a book
at a library in school
sounds louder and louder.

OUTLAW

I've ridden with wanted men.
Sometimes I had to shoot my own horse.
I keep a lock of her blonde hair
in a tin can
buried somewhere in the mine.
I dig around in my saddle bag
to find some whiskey
to feed the salty desires.
I hang up my spurs
to become one of you,
but the past is outlined
with so many pennies.

PLAY THE HAND

The word survivor always sounds good—
Cancer survivor.
Drug survivor.
Love survivor.
Taking a beating can be beautiful
at the end
When you stand on the stage,
just standing.
You don't have to do anything else.
War survivor.
Prison survivor.
Religious survivor.
It takes a long time for a rock to become smooth.
The risks are worth it.

PORTRAIT

Paint me a portrait
that outlines the shape of a dog.
She wouldn't let me get one.
"Too much hair everywhere in my house,"
she would say.
I go to pet my brother's dog out of courtesy at his house
and its face feels mangy—
the runny nose,
the shedding hair,
and the lick of slobber.
Mom,
paint me this portrait,
so something else can make my life
unclean.

CANDLES

A cowboy,
an artist,
and a tiger
were what I wanted to be
when I was five years old.
As I look at the candles today
on the cake,
those dreams
are still worth blowing out.

THE CHASE

Grandfather,
deal me an ace
so I can feel worthy
to be at ease
being alone.

With the flick of your wrist,
the card could come,
the one I've been chasing
in too many dreams.

It's often times thought about
when I'm on a train.
It lets my manic depression
be split down the tracks.

And everything seems so clear on the train,
my death,
my love for the girl at the next stop.
If not her,
then something better.

Behind the train
one page of poetry blows,
everlasting.

chiwan choi

THE KILLS

somewhat as if he'd forgotten
who he was   or rather remembering
himself wrong   galloped is the wrong word
one i most relate to a horse   the dog jumped
up and down in place
by the couch determined to
throw off the invisible rider
until we laughed around him until
we cried.

he gave me my first moment, then,
of stillness   his four feet
distanced from each other with such
precision that balance was just a matter
of will   the left edge of his cone
caught against the open door   his shaved
eyes circled with stitches holding
his eyelids open   waiting to move
waiting to move.

and the second to go was his sister
who watched that night from the backyard
her nose steaming a hole on the sliding
glass door   barking so we couldn't hear
on her 6th birthday in the valley
near a restaurant looking like a puzzle
sent by an aunt in connecticut   how there
was no falling in death   no blood in death   no screaming
or crying in death, but only breathing no more.

and in a few days, i will touch
the part of me that i have forgotten,
on the freeway into the sun tapping
the roof of my wife's gray car with
the fingers of my left hand   sunglasses
covering the teary eyes for dramatic effect.
the brown hair on the seat picked
and held to my nose to smell the familiarity
of filth left in my wake.
number three   number three   they come and go
in threes.

but they are no longer deaths.
they are kills.
number one is my daughter.
i watched *jerry maguire* on the couch
eating pringles while waiting for her to be aborted
on santa monica boulevard.
number two is cassie
and telling the vet to throw her body away
as i drove to the airport for a trip to new york.
and number three stands two inches
from the garage door now
wanting to know what happens if he takes
one more blind step forward,
and takes it   a soft thud of his head against
the garage.

driving into the sun, i imagine,
and too close to the white lines on the left
side of my lane, forcing fingers to fumble
through dials of less broken voices.
i will no longer run from the ones
i am called to destroy.
and i wrap my arms around his smelly body

the hair itching at my lip,
loving once again the nature of my life:
to find
to love
to neglect
to kill
to learn how to put into words
such moments when nothing
moves.

katherine paull

SATURDAY NIGHT

I've been waiting for my life for a while now.
I edit it as I wait.
I erase people and places
so I can slide open new doors
that may want me inside.
Pathetic.
The phone rings and it's
an automatic telemarketing call.
I'm waiting for something else.
I have a loose-lipped life, full of opinion
smacking with shame.

Those full-lived folks hum like bees,
sporting classy jackets,
pie baker moms humming ditties to teeming tribes.
I want to feel of use.

I DON'T LIVE IN A TOWN

I get tired of being the opposition,
tired of saying, "Look you stupid ego driven mindsots,
a canyon is not a town,
just as a cow is not a horse,
a bird is not a deer,
a peach is not a plum,
today is not tomorrow at this moment."
I have lived in cities named after English earls
and cities that call themselves saints.
I've lived in a town with a "boro" on its end.
I have lived by water and cornfields,
creeks and hills, and I didn't need to call them towns.
When a drunk staggers out of the bar
I drive by every day
and he misses the curve on his Harley,
he moves up the road to the cemetery.
A bar and a cemetery are not a town.
They are conveniences.

ROUND ONE

My head is a mush tank.
I sort of slept last night with a cat and a daughter.
We were all restless in our distress.
When I walked into the bedroom,
the daughter looked like an emanation
from a Poe story: splotch of pink in a white bed
in a white room, lying in misery.
No jazz. No light.
Just a three barf hangover
and a jilted lover
and gushers of tears,
orificial tears too big to mop.
Sad sad tears.

I'd like to spit out my own juices into the perpetrator's eye.
"So why'd you marry her, asshole?"
I'd taunt. "Little weasel wimp."

But she and I are good girls.
We take our punches lying down.

ARTISTS WHO KILL THEMSELVES

Tonight someone told me
that some people should kill themselves
so we don't have to listen to them anymore.
They should just die and get it over with.
We had been reading Sylvia Plath.
Anne Sexton's poem on Sylvia's death
was more depressing than
the plethora of Plath's early self-eulogies.
And then Robert Lowell killed himself, too.
They all knew each other.
What a wallow they must have had together
in glum silence after intoxicated enlightenment.

I went with Phil to see Robert de la Rocha
before he died. He lay on a couch
too feeble to move more than a skeletal hand.
"Don't worry, I'm fine," he reassured.
He wanted it that way.
He thought he was Christ in his starvation high.
Death was his savior.
He wasn't sick, just crazy,
while his smiling parents made shadowy circles
in the kitchen.

bios

ALAN BERMAN teaches web, programming, and office applications at El Camino Real High School in Woodland Hills, CA. He has been published in *Mosaic, Literary Magazine Review, Guitar Review,* and *VUEPoint.* He lives in Los Angeles.

ALICIA RUSKIN, by day, tirelessly promotes and celebrates the artistic endeavors of her clients; by night, she entertains her own. On the weekend, she likes to sleep.

AMY SLOMOVITS moved to Los Angeles 10 years ago from Cleveland, Ohio, to be in the business we call "Show." Currently, she ducks away once a week from her life as a talent manager to get a weekly fix of life within the literati. She is best known for her endless college journals that portray the angst of a 20 year old with zero responsibility.

CAROLINE HORTON is British born and bred, a true New Yorker and currently addicted to the weather in Los Angeles where she lives with her daughter and Siamese cat. She has been a traveling journalist throughout Europe and is currently working on her first novel.

CARRIE WHITE is a mother of five, a grandmother of eight, a lifetime Beverly Hills salon owning superstar hairdresser, a professional photographer, a published poet with a an autobiography in progress, a chemical dependency recovery speaker for 21 years, a world traveler, and a student.

CHIWAN CHOI is Los Angeles, by way of Paraguay and Korea. He is a founding editor of WEDNESDAY, this incredible magazine you are reading, and author of two books of poetry, *dogfuzz on the asscrack/time out of space* and *lo-fidelity lovesongs.* He has returned to Los Angeles after receiving his MFA in Dramatic Writing from the Tisch School at NYU. He lives with his really hot wife and a series of tragic dogs.

CHRIS KERR, an avid *I Love Lucy* fan, was born and lives in Los Angeles. She's married to a very understanding husband, and is a mother to a wise and spirited long hair Chihuahua.

CHRIS SHEARER is an enthusiast and lives in a building in Los Angeles. He is an actor in a whole bunch of films that nobody ever sees and he is not bitter about it. Some of them weren't so good. The last one is great. It's called *In This Short Life* and Chris is hoping other enthusiasts will go see it. Chris grew up in the back of a pickup truck in upstate New York and believe me, it's cold enough to freeze the nuts off a squirrel up there. Fuckin' cold, man. Green, though. Someday he will have a house up there—one with a heater in it.

CHRISTY DUSABLON is a starving student who, as the cliche goes, likes to get drunk, have sex, and write. That may not even be a cliche. But she is happy right now and finds, for the first time in a long time, that all her relationships are in an excellent place. She would like to stay here for a while.

CONRAD ROMO is a native Los Angelino. He is the producer/host of two dynamic short story and poetry reading events; *Tongue & Groove*, and *Palabrazilla*. He is short, stocky and swarthy. He would like to be thought of as a ladies man, a man's man and a dog's best friend. Well, at least dogs like him. He is compiling a collection of short stories and a cd.

CRAIG BERGMAN thinks he's hardcore New York, but he's just an LA poet who likes to wear a Yankees cap and remember the good old days in Coney Island and girl watching in Brooklyn when he didn't have to shed so much blood on the page.

ELIZABETH BRADLEY was raised in San Francisco and San Diego. She is a writer, designer and recovering lawyer, currently living in Los Angeles.

ELLEN KIMMEL is a social worker who has been studying poetry for over ten years. She is originally from Brooklyn and Lawn Giland. When she is not writing poetry, she is throwing pots at the Bitter Root Pottery Studio.

FRANCINE TAYLOR has written screenplays, fiction, non-fiction and poetry. She has also had a number of short plays produced in NOHO Non-Equity Theater. She writes regularly for greencine.com, an independent film website, and loves interviewing filmmakers. She is very happy to be included in the latest issue of WEDNESDAY.

JUDETH ODEN is addicted to *Millenium* on DVD. She has enjoyed success as an off-off-Broadway playwright, has an MFA in Dramatic Writing from NYU, teaches an arts and literacy program for high school students, and is a founding editor of WEDNESDAY.

JUSTIN KLIPPEL is a native Angelino. He is 25 years old and a student. He plans on becoming a history teacher. He loves intensity, 1950's pinup girls, and shamanic tendencies. He is working on his first collection of poems.

KATE CRASH is Kate Crash. Punk rockin' rockin' roller Ready TO TAKE ON YOU AND YOUR BAD REVIEWS…Nothing is cooler than sucking…so please place your lips on the page and suck!!! And remember…please tip and SHE LOVES YOU!!!!

KATHARINE PAULL is a part time literacy coach and former high school English teacher. A former resident of Virginia and North Carolina, she has been living in Kagel Canyon, CA since 1970.

KATHY GRAF is an actress, working in television and film. She has also done over a hundred commercials and voice-overs. She started writing three years ago working on a one-woman show, *Surviving David*, which she performed in Los Angeles, garnering great reviews. The show was invited to participate in the New York International Fringe Festival in the summer of 2005, winning an Award of Excellence for Outstanding Solo Show. She has recently completed writing her first full-length play and the screenplay version of *Surviving David*.

KATY MELODY is a writer and psychotherapist. She lives in Los Angeles with her husband, actor, Andrew Parks.

LAUREL BENTON is a Valley Girl born and bred, and still living in LA (because the natives never leave) and when she was 19, she marched right up to Gregory Peck and shook his hand because he, after all, WAS Atticus Finch.

LEDA ROGERS conceived the term "eclectic creator" to describe herself. She loves to go rock hounding for semi-precious stones with her dog Scooby. This Actor, Writer, Graphic Designer, Silversmith, Brooklyn original, now lives to create in Los Angeles. She is working on her novel, *Brooklyn*.

LESLIE WARD was born in 1958, in Lincoln, Nebraska, moving to Los Angeles a year later where she has lived ever since, save for a brief stint in Colorado where she fell in love with the mountains while diligently honing her waitressing skills. Leslie continues to live and work in Los Angeles, selling big books with pretty covers, lots of pictures and very few words. She lives with her wildly talented artist husband, Gary, their unbelievably adorable son, Henry, and their fabulous dog, Ed.

LINDA MCMILLIN PYLE was born in St. Paul, Minnesta and graduated from the University of Minnesota. She has published numerous travel articles and photographic essays. She is the author of *Peaks, Palms & Picnics: Day Journeys in the Mountains & Deserts of Palm Springs & the Coachella Valley* and *Pacific Peaks & Picnics: Day Journeys in San Diego County.* She loves to walk dirt roads, singletrack trails and boreens with her husband, T.M. They live in San Clemente, California with Seger and Columbo, their Tonkinese cats.

LUCY MCCUSKER is a native Angelino and has been a hair stylist extraordinaire for a long ass time. She is currently trying to put together the million crazy stories from her life into a novel so the Hollywood types holding guns to her head can steal it and make buckets of cash. And her new house is friggin' cool.

MARGUERITE LAMBRINOS is a writer, a teacher, and lives up in the canyon.

MARIA CRISTINA JIMÉNEZ wishes she had clever things to say, but alas, all that comes out is that she's grateful to be writing every day and to be part of LA's merry band of artists. Writing and teaching/practicing yoga keeps her from spiraling into herself.

MELINDA MCGRAW, originally from Cambridge, MA, is an actress who briefly studied at Bennington College before training at The Royal Academy of Dramatic Arts in London. Recently her original pursuit of writing has come to and dusted itself off. She lives in Los Angeles in a passionate, joyous and messy household with her husband, daughter and two dogs. She is also the author of *SKINLESS*, a chapbook.

ROBERT CARROLL, M.D. is a poet and psychiatrist. He is in private practice in Westwood and is on the faculty at UCLA's Dept. of Psychiatry. He has published many poems, stories and chapters in the psychiatric/medical and poetry literatures and is the author of more than 30 chapbooks of poetry. He was a member of the Los Angeles Slam Team for three years. He currently serves as Vice President of the National Association for Poetry Therapy.

ROBIN BURROWS was a Mormon when she was six. She rides a paint horse named after a man who couldn't last in this world, but inspires much poetry. Now she is learning to cut cattle on her new pride, Reminics Chic. She wears sexy suede chaps and has suddenly, at long last, fallen in love.

TERI GOLDMAN is a writer, a social worker, and a yoga enthusiast. A native Angelino, she dreamed of being the next Pat Benatar. The disappointment of this dashed aspiration has fueled a lifetime of poetry. Her writing has appeared in *ONTHEBUS*, *The Art of the Brain*, and the *International Journal of Healing and Caring*. She is writing her first novel and completing a collection of short poems.

THOMAS NATICK has worked as a writer, producer and director over the past ten years. He co-wrote Turner Pictures' animated feature *Cats Don't Dance*, which won the Annie Award for Best Picture in 1997. He was also nominated for two Emmy Awards and won the Silver Angel for producing and directing Disney's animated series *101 Dalmatians*. He is currently writing and producing two live action features for the Zanuck Company and has begun work on his first novel.

TIM SILVER was born and grew up in Ohio, journeyed in Europe, Africa, and Asia, studied film, theater, and literature in London and New York City. He works freelance in film and television production. He lives with his wife, Margarita, in Santa Monica, California.

CPSIA information can be obtained at www.ICGtesting.com
Printed in the USA
BVOW11s1440050915

416533BV00004B/14/P

9 780941 017725